BBC FOOD CHECK

BBC Food Check

Your Practical Guide to Safe Food

DAVID EDWARDS of the
Food Hygiene Bureau
and PETER BAZALGETTE

BBC BOOKS

Acknowledgements

The authors wish to thank the following for their valuable help in preparing
this book: Annette Anderson, Andy Benstead of Barnet Department of
Health, the staff of Bazal Productions (particularly Karen Flower), Debbie
Brown of The Consumers' Association, Eileen Edwards (an Environmental
Health Officer herself, who contributed many ideas), Vicky Ewart who
helped research Chapter 9, Alison Field who helped research Chapter 1,
Alexander Flinder of the Alexander Flinder Ashley Partnership, the staff of
the Food Hygiene Bureau (particularly Nicky and Sam), Dr Richard Gilbert
(Director of the Food Hygiene Laboratory at Colindale), the Health Educa-
tion Council, Nicky Hughes who helped research Chapter 7, The Institute
of Environmental Health Officers (particularly Linda Allen and Hilary King),
Brian Lawson (formerly of the Cranfield Institute of Technology), Dr John
Newman, Gabrielle O'Connor who helped research Chapter 6, Dr Colin
Smithers of the PA Consultancy Technology Division, Alan Stennard of
Camden Department of Health and the Environmental Services Division of
Wandsworth Borough Council.

Published by BBC Books,
A division of BBC Enterprises Ltd
Woodlands, 80 Wood Lane, London W12 0TT

First published 1989

© The Authors 1989

ISBN 0 563 20789 2

Typeset in 10/12½ pt Times
by Ace Filmsetting Ltd, Frome, Somerset
Printed and bound in Great Britain by Richard Clays Ltd, Bungay, Suffolk
Cover printed by Richard Clays Ltd, Norwich

CONTENTS

Introduction
The Global Café

'FOR SOME YEARS the public has been obsessed by additives. Until recently the real threat to our health – food poisoning – has been practically ignored.'

Dr Verner Wheelock, Head of the Food Policy Research Unit, Bradford University

'We are now experiencing the worst food poisoning epidemic ever in the United Kingdom.'

Professor Richard Lacey, Microbiology Department, Leeds University

'The rise in Salmonella enteritidis cases in 1988 was enormous. The farmer needs to take more care to ensure that meat and eggs aren't coming into the home infected. Meanwhile the consumer is unfortunately the last line of defence at the moment.'

Bob Tanner, Chief Executive of The Institute of Environmental Health Officers

'Education may be the most important key. If consumers understand the problems they will make sure that the preparation of food in the home is safely done and will pressurise the food trade to do even better.'

Sir Donald Acheson, Chief Medical Officer, Department of Health

'All the demands that modern society puts on food – to extend the shelf life, make it look more natural, make it immediately edible with the minimum of cooking – all these add to the problems of food poisoning.'

Dr Edward Manning, Executive Vice-President of the US National Association of Federal Veterinarians

Food poisoning is a major problem – there is no doubt about that – and it is a growing one. Whose fault is it? Is the food industry to blame for selling us rotten food, or are we to blame for mishandling it? That is the current debate in Britain. But whether the fault lies with the food industry or our own ignorance we still need to know far more about food poisoning and how to avoid it. Other books can and should point the finger at some of those who supply our food. This book has a different function – only by learning the simple rules of food hygiene can we protect ourselves – from both our own bad practices and those of the food suppliers. That is our single purpose . . . to provide a practical guide to safe food.

If you choose to read the whole book at one sitting you will find much to stimulate you, much to surprise you and a little that might even horrify you. Alternatively, with the aid of the index at the back, you can just as easily refer to specific topics as and when you find it necessary.

These days we may know how to drive a car, use a telephone and operate a computer but we are woefully ignorant about how food is produced and how it functions. We may well understand a certain amount about what constitutes a healthy diet but we know little of food chemistry and practically nothing of the causes of food poisoning. We were not always so ignorant. Many civilisations, including our own until well into this century, had strict rules about food safety which food handlers – normally the women – learnt. Now an all-providing convenience food industry has removed the need for everyone to know how to cook. And the sad truth is that with the loss of our cooking skills has gone the knowledge of how to handle food correctly. We urgently need to regain that knowledge.

Before the advent of convenience foods we shopped for fresh food every day, and cooked every day too. If we handled food badly then we poisoned only ourselves and our own family. Nowadays if a mass supplier of food makes a mistake he can poison thousands of us. In that sense we are all sitting down at the same table to eat. If there is something wrong in the kitchen of this 'global café' it affects us all, unless – and here's the rub – we know how to store, prepare and heat the food in such a way as to protect ourselves.

Is a woman's place in the home, and more particularly, in the kitchen? Most women would bridle at the rank prejudice of such an idea. It is now accepted that women work and pursue careers. Indeed, in this past decade of high unemployment, women have often been the *only* people working in many households. The catch is that the majority of households still rely on women to shop and cook (a recent Government survey found that three-quarters of the women questioned carried out the household food shopping). As a result many women have to rely on convenience products. Even if their mothers taught them to cook they are unlikely to pass those skills on to their children. Without real cooking (as opposed to reheating) going on in the home, there are no opportunities for such tuition. While the suppliers of convenience foods undoubtedly fulfil a useful social function they have still had a devastating effect. Tragically few of us have a thorough knowledge of food any more.

If we are not to learn about food at home, why not at school? What about home economics? Home economics – or domestic science, as it is sometimes called – is unfortunately very much a poor relation in the school curriculum. Provisional figures for children taking the new GCSE exams in 1988 reveal the following:

Home economics	177654
Art and design	218775
English language	638636
Mathematics	653716

And the story is much the same for the most recent numbers of A level candidates, from 1986:

Social science (incl. dom. sci.)	7300
English	39100
Mathematics	54690

(Source: Department of Education)

The minority of children who did take the new GCSE exam in the summer of 1988 would have had to answer questions such as these from the syllabus of the Southern Examining Group:

Give a reason for each of the following statements:

- A frozen chicken must be thoroughly thawed before cooking.
- Pets should not be allowed to eat from the family's crockery.

Suggest, with reasons, two ways you can be sure that the food you buy is fresh.

Pupils taking A level domestic science the same summer would have had to answer this question from the Associated Examination Board:

Food poisoning appears to be on the increase in the United Kingdom. Discuss this statement in relation to the reasons for this increase and the strategies that could be adopted in order to reduce the incidence of food poisoning.

But very few schoolchildren saw either of these exam papers or had undertaken the studies necessary to answer them. Even those pupils who did sit the exam did not have to answer many questions about food. Food is only a part of the home economics syllabus. Brenda Smith, a lecturer in home economics at Trent Polytechnic, points out that as the need for children to learn about food grows, the subject is declining – once again because of changes in the way a woman's role is perceived: 'Before the days of equal opportunities most girls spent half a day a week studying the subject, and it covered all aspects of food hygiene, economics of food buying, healthy foods, safety in the kitchen, storage and so on. Nowadays if the school has it on the general curriculum at all kids would only get about one hour a week. But it could be neglected completely – boys very rarely do anything on the subject.'

We do not need to get bogged down here in a tedious discussion as to what a woman's role in the family should be. The plain fact is that at least one adult, and preferably all adults, within a family need to know how to handle food. The parents of today's schoolchildren – by and large – cannot teach such skills because they have never acquired them. That leaves school. The Department of Education is currently preparing a report about the future of home economics in the national curriculum. It might be included in a subject called 'design and technology' which would also include art, design and business studies. We can judge the relative importance of home economics in the new scheme of things by the fact that the subject's umbrella title (Design and Technology) gives no hint that it has anything to do with food. The only good news on the horizon is that from September 1989 the national science curriculum will include some information for 11 to 14-year-olds about harmful food bacteria. About time.

We had a lengthy discussion about whether to use the phrase 'safe food' on the front of this book. Some thought it had connotations of 'safe sex' and Aids and that such a suggestion was unfortunate. But because VD and Aids are such a problem every schoolchild receives sex education. Far, far more people suffer from food poisoning than Aids or VD. So why don't *all* schoolchildren receive food education? There would be no resistance from them – it's a lot more fun than maths.

It is ironic that all students starting at catering college have an induction week teaching them about safe food handling. They are not allowed near food until they understand correct kitchen practice and the dangers of food poisoning. It is ironic because we *all* work with food but few of us are given such training.

At its most extreme, handling food properly is a matter of life and death. The Jews have built food hygiene into their religious laws – the survival of their race depended on it. That is how important it was to them. The Jewish ghettos of eastern Europe often escaped the worst effects of cholera and typhoid epidemics even though the diseases were raging nearby. Their enemies put their good fortune down to sorcery but it is commonly thought today that their religious laws and practices protected them. If you have never read the Kosher laws you would be surprised to find that, with the exception of a few particularly obscure rules, they read like a standard textbook on food hygiene. Many of the rules, by the way, are derived from the Old Testament which Christians ostensibly subscribe to as well. These are some of the broad areas covered by Kosher law:

- *Clean and unclean animals* Pork and shellfish, both a common source of poisoning, are among the prohibited foods.

- *Products of unclean beings* These include the eggs of 'unclean birds', those who have been following the Salmonella saga will be interested to note.

- *Slaughtering* This is a point in the processing of food at which contamination can easily, and often does, occur.

- *Defective animals* It is prohibited to eat diseased beasts or those that have died from natural causes.

- *Food containing worms or insects* This is prohibited, but of course only covers what is visible to the naked eye.

- *Cleansing of utensils* We tend to forget that the main reason for washing-up is to kill bacteria, not just to remove bits of food.

- *Regular washing* One cause of food poisoning today is the food handler who has not washed after a visit to the lavatory.

The Talmud – the compilation of ancient Jewish law – lays down a number of these rules, along with others relating to hygiene. Among them are the following:

- Latrines to be situated outside a camp.
- Bath-houses to be built first in Jewish settlements, even before a synagogue.
- Water used should not be stagnant – it must be 'living water' such as rain, spring water or river water.
- Any liquid left uncovered overnight should not be drunk.

■ Separate sets of crockery always to be used for different purposes.

One cannot help coming to the conclusion that if we all prac-
tised the strict rules of a Kosher household there would be no
food poisoning problem at all today. Rabbi Lionel Blue, familiar to those who listen to Radio 4's *Today* programme, says that
he has always been shocked at how few men wash their hands
before leaving a public lavatory. Whenever he washes his
hands thoroughly he then ritually sprays three jets of water on
to each hand and says, 'Blessed are you, Lord our God, who
commands us to wash our hands.' Hygiene and religion are
one and the same for him. Rabbi Blue also describes the confusion caused by modern factory farming methods which mix
foods in such a way as to make it almost impossible to apply
the simple food definitions from the Talmud. To avoid endless
wrangling and heart-searching as to what is and is not Kosher
many Jews are becoming vegetarians. They will be none the
worse for that – harmful bacteria prefer meat to most other
sorts of food (see Chapter 3, page 44). And these Jews are in
good company – orthodox Buddhists cannot eat animals that
have been slaughtered.

Muslims and Hindus also have strict laws about food.
Muslims are prohibited from eating pork and food made with
blood, such as black pudding. Hindu law has been particularly
concerned with preparation and storage. Peeling and slicing
were believed to open the food to contamination; cooked rice
left overnight was 'unclean'; ready-cooked dishes for re-use
were frowned upon (consumers of TV dinners take note); food
that had been sniffed at by a dog or cat was also unclean.

It is often said we live in an uncertain and ungodly age –
nowhere is this truer than the kitchen. In an era of uncertainty
people are very susceptible to confusion and even panic. In late
1988 and early 1989 we saw several instances of this. Even more
worrying are those who take advantage of this public anxiety to
further their own interests. Let us give you just two examples.

A certain Water Authority was fed-up with the healthy
image bottled mineral waters had achieved at the expense of

tap water. So they did a simple analysis of both, knowing full well what they would find. Their tap water had far fewer bacteria in it than bottled mineral waters. They released the results to a few MPs who attacked bottled waters in the House of Commons. The story duly appeared in the newspapers.

What is the truth of the matter? Of course bottled mineral waters have bacteria in them – they are a natural, unprocessed product, straight from an environment teeming with harmless bacteria (much as our own bodies are). Of course tap water contained fewer bacteria – tap water has had chemicals pumped into it to kill as many organisms as possible. It is utterly lifeless and usually tastes like it too.

The other example arose during the recent concern about Listeria. The Government had discovered that some soft, rinded cheeses like Brie and Camembert had relatively high concentrations of the bacterium, Listeria monocytogenes. They finally concluded (as other experts had before them) that this represented a particular threat to pregnant women. It is now thought that the bacterium is a significant cause of miscarriages and stillbirths.

Dairy Crest is the massive cheese-making arm of the Milk Marketing Board. They make some soft, rinded cheeses – Lymeswold for one – and were presumably worried that the Government warning might harm their sales. They were immediately quoted in a newspaper to the effect that the Government's warning only related to cheeses made from unpasteurised milk. Subsequently, two Government Ministers also gave the impression that unpasteurised cheeses were a particular problem. They were all wrong. In fact the worst outbreak of Listeria poisoning (in which 37 people died) was caused by a Swiss cheese made from *pasteurised* milk. But the damage was done and in the confusion that ensued small cheese-makers making cheese the traditional way, from unpasteurised milk, suffered a drop in sales.

These two stories exemplify how, because of our ignorance of food, we are vulnerable to misinformation. And they also serve to remind us that we all buy our food and drink from mass suppliers . . . if there is something wrong in the kitchen of

this global café of ours then we all suffer. What is worse is that
the very act of mass supply brings with it dangers that did not
previously exist. Dr Edward Manning, the distinguished veteri-
narian in the United States whom we quoted at the beginning
of this Introduction, puts it this way:

'Food poisoning bacteria are increasing due to our advanc-
ing technology. Decades ago milk, meat and vegetables
were consumed fresh, close to their source and in their
original state. Now animals are shipped around, their feed
is imported and shipped around, the animals are cut up
into nearly-ready-to-eat pieces and shipped around again.
The food, once it is brought home, is mixed with other
food, chopped, frozen and unfrozen much more than
before. At every stage more contamination and cross-
contamination can occur.

'On the farm where I was brought up we caught a
chicken, killed it, plunged it into boiling water to take the
feathers off (coincidentally killing any bacteria on its surface) and then cooked it thoroughly. Nowadays a chicken
in a poultry processing factory will be mixed with tens of
thousands of others at every stage. Cross-contamination is
rife. The chicken is then handled many times by hands
and machines leading to further cross-contamination.
Then it's kept in unreliable refrigeration and chilled.

'The whole chain from farm to table has become more
complex and at each stage there is more chance of intro-
ducing dirt into the food product.'

Those are the processes going on in the farms and kitchens
serving our global café. Meanwhile we eat more and more of
the high-risk foods. More than half our chickens contain
Salmonella. But whereas 50 years ago each of us ate 5 lb of
chicken every year, we now eat 40 lb.

What of the people who work in the global café? If we are
lamentably ignorant of food, will they be any better? Here are
three cautionary tales.

In 1985 it was revealed that glasses of beer in some British pubs would be alarmingly high in bacteria from human faeces. An investigation revealed that customers were failing to wash their hands after visiting the lavatory. When their glasses were refilled beer spilled down the side (where their fingers had been) into the slops tray. Against the rules laid down by the brewers the publicans were then recyling the slops – hence the contamination. A 1989 survey of beer glasses in Somerset also found high levels of bacteria. *Casual staff in pubs will rarely, if ever, have had food hygiene training.*

In 1987 two customers reported food poisoning from sandwiches bought from different branches of a British sandwich bar chain. The problem was traced back to a kitchen worker stripping chickens. He had a festering wound on his hand that was contaminating the chicken. *He had never been trained in food handling, nor does the law require him to be.*

In Manchester in 1989, a woman reported suffering a raging fever, diarrhoea and vomiting after eating a takeaway. The problem was traced to some 'chicken nuggets' she had eaten. They were contaminated by Listeria and had not been cooked thoroughly. The staff may or may not have had food hygiene training but *it is not usual for staff in a takeaway to have received any education in food science.*

Everyone, including the people we might assume to be 'professionals', needs to know about safe food. The more we rely on mass-supplied, pre-prepared foods the greater is the risk to our health and the greater our need to understand food.

Consider how our lunchtime habits have changed and how often we now buy sandwiches. (Government research being carried out at the moment – as yet confidential – may reveal that sandwiches are a much greater source of food poisoning than we have hitherto realised.)

Consider, too, how our shopping habits have changed in recent years. Instead of shopping every day at a corner shop for fresh food, we shop once a week and expect the food to keep. A 1988 survey carried out by the Ministry of Agriculture, Fisheries and Food confirms this:

■ Two-thirds of adults shop only *once* a week for perishable food.

■ Four-fifths of shoppers buy pre-packed chilled or frozen items.

There are so many different technologies at work to bring us our food. Each one produces food which needs to be handled differently and has a different storage life. How much do you really understand about the different food processes? Try yourself out with the processes mentioned below. In each case ask yourself on what principles the process works and how the food should be treated when you get it home:

■ Canning
■ Drying
■ Freezing
■ Cook-chill
■ Sous-Vide

How did you do? Did you know, for instance, that:

Canning is a process in which fresh food is sealed from the outside in a can and sterilised by heating to around 120°C, that this kills any bacteria so no preservatives are necessary and that the food can last for two to three years? Did you also know that John West and several other companies are now selling long-life meals in flat packs; in other words, that canned food does not have to come in a can?

Drying is the removal of water from food which protects it against deterioration but can adversely affect colour, flavour and vitamin content. Not all dried food can reabsorb water satisfactorily.

Freezing requires the food to be reduced to a temperature of −18°C which is the temperature your domestic freezer should not rise above. Flavour, colour and vitamins are generally preserved but texture can be damaged.

Cook-chill allows food to be prepared in advance and then, within 90 minutes, it is blast chilled to a temperature strictly between 0° and 3°C. It should be reheated, within five days, to a temperature of at least 70°C and consumed within two hours.

Sous-Vide puts food raw or part-cooked into plastic bags which are sealed under vacuum to remove all the air. The food may then be cooked or pasteurised (heat-treated) while in the bag. Like cook-chill, it is then blast chilled to between 0° and 3°C. The other rules as to its handling are similar to those for cook-chill foods.

If you are entirely honest with yourself you did not know all that, did you? If you did, then you are probably a food technologist or a research chemist. It does begin to seem that those are the sort of skills we need to handle the foods that technology is providing us with nowadays.

And that brings us back to the purpose of this book: to set out, in a simple and digestible way, the things we need to know to survive in the global café. We very much hope that the advice it contains will help you minimise the chances of food poisoning occurring in your home.

1 WHAT IS IT LIKE TO BE POISONED?

Gippy Tummy, Basra Belly, the Kathmandu Quickstep, Delhi
Belly, the Rangoon Runs, Hong Kong Dog, the Ho Chi Minhs,
Tokyo Trots, Montezuma's Revenge, the Aztec Twostep . . .
most of the popular names for food poisoning echo our colonial past, when sons of Empire went abroad and came into
contact with strange foods and the even stranger bacteria in
them. The results could be explosive. But now we are beginning
to be concerned about colonial matters nearer home – the
colonisation of our stomachs by bacteria that are present in our
own environment. We say *beginning* to be concerned because
until recently most of us have not given the subject of food
poisoning a second thought. Then all of a sudden isolated
cases are featured in gory detail on the front pages of tabloid
newspapers. Our most common reaction is probably 'how
unfortunate', and we subconsciously feel it has little to do with
us. But that gut reaction to the gut reactions of others is a mis-
taken one. Any one of us could become a victim at any time.

To find out how serious food poisoning can be, we now
invite you to read our 'Casebook'. It contains 10 incidents of
food poisoning involving both adults and children. Some suffered minor upset stomachs, some were very ill and in two
cases there were deaths. Establishing the exact cause of food
poisoning is frequently difficult and sometimes impossible. So
in some of the stories that follow we have only the suspicions
of the victims to go on, though they were all clearly ill. Many of
these people wrote to BBC2's *Food and Drink* programme. In
one case the names have been changed for personal reasons.

CASE 1: CATHERINE AND THE OX LIVER

Bernice and David Clark live in the Ribble Valley near
Clitheroe. In 1989 they reached the final of the *Food and Drink*

programme's national cookery competition. Bernice insisted on cooking the stuffing separately from her roast chicken so as to be absolutely sure the fowl was thoroughly roasted and free of Salmonella. The reason became clear when we spoke to her.

Bernice and David had been married for 17 years and had tried to have children of their own for some time but without success. They had been turned down for adoption by agencies in Manchester who said they were too old. So they applied to be foster parents and eventually the Local Authority in Ribble sent them a baby – Catherine – who was only seven weeks old and had just been taken into care. During the fostering period Bernice used to take Catherine to see her natural mother at a nursery. It was just after one of these visits that what Bernice describes as 'a seven-month nightmare' began.

David looked at Catherine and said, 'She's not well – she's very pasty-looking.' And sure enough, shortly afterwards she began to vomit. Bernice was surprised because Catherine was normally a very healthy child. But that night she was sick seven times. The doctor came and said it was just a stomach bug and she would get over it.

The following morning Catherine had obviously had diarrhoea all night and Bernice remembers an overpowering smell of yeast in her room. She was really anxious and she summoned the Health Visitor who took a sample from Catherine's nappy. By now the sickness had stopped but the diarrhoea continued. A week later she had a letter from the local Environmental Health Office revealing that Catherine was suffering from a rare strain of Salmonella, found in ox's liver, called 'Mileagridef'. Bernice was devastated and was immediately plagued with feelings of guilt even though she wasn't sure when or where Catherine had contracted the Salmonella.

For the next seven months she had to take samples from Catherine's nappy *three times daily* and send them for analysis. Catherine was soon well again and she began to put on weight. After seven months baby Catherine was given the all-clear and today she is a chatty, happy three-year-old who knows nothing of what happened in her first year of life. She has now been formally adopted by Bernice and David.

They never did establish where the bug came from – Bernice's home was cleared and no other children at the day nursery suffered any problems. Bernice and David were always careful about hygiene in the kitchen but now they describe themselves as fanatical.

CASE 2: THE RUSSIAN CREAM PUDDING

Len and Margaret Russell opened a seaside restaurant in the West Country in May 1988. In the first four weeks business was already picking up and they had high hopes for their new venture. Len's mother was staying the weekend and made a Russian cream pudding for Sunday lunch – Len and Margaret welcomed someone else doing the cooking for once.

Len became ill that same evening with vomiting and diarrhoea. Margaret dismissed it as a minor tummy bug and the following day treated herself to a bowl of the Russian cream pudding. That evening she fell ill as well. Now they were both helpless in bed with Len's mother (at the age of 80) nursing them. 'I could quite happily have died – I never thought I could feel so ill,' says Len.

'We both felt absolutely ghastly. We were hallucinating and having the most frightful nightmares. The doctor came to look at us and quite honestly didn't take too much notice – I think he found it quite amusing that we were both lying in bed feeling so lousy,' recalls Margaret. In fact they were still ill in a week's time – Len had lost a stone and a half and Margaret a stone. The doctor returned to take samples. The verdict from the Environmental Health Officer shortly afterwards was . . . Salmonella. After a range of tests (including an exhaustive examination of their dog, Montgomery) it was discovered that the pudding was full of Salmonella, as were two remaining eggs from the batch Len's mother had used to make it.

Their restaurant had now been closed for over a week. Then came the bombshell – the Health Officer announced it had to remain closed until they were clear of the Salmonella (which was entiritidis phage type 4). 'We felt like lepers –

unclean,' says Margaret. The Health Officer, though, did his best to put them at their ease – he accepted a cup of tea from Margaret, which made her feel less of an outcast.

It took seven weeks for their systems to get rid of the Salmonella. They lost £1500 a week and are still trying to sort out compensation from their insurance company. Meanwhile, although Len's mother was also found to be Salmonella-positive she somehow managed to escape illness, as did the restaurant's customers. 'Thank God *we* ate the pudding and didn't give it to our clientele,' says Len. When they were preparing to open up once again for the summer season in 1989 Margaret had adopted a new culinary regime. She wouldn't serve fresh egg puddings unless they were to be cooked at high temperatures. And she makes her lemon meringue pie with dried egg white. As for Len, he does not eat eggs at all any more.

Case 3: Daniel's fried egg

Victoria Bignold was cooking a quick supper for her four children one September evening in 1988 at their South London home. Fried sausage and baked potatoes were on the menu but Daniel, her 10-year-old, insisted on adding a fried egg to his meal. The following day, at the Dulwich art gallery where Victoria works, she received a call from Daniel's school – could she pick him up because he was unwell?

As soon as she got him home Daniel started to vomit violently and diarrhoea set in soon afterwards. The following evening he fainted while sitting on the lavatory and then again in bed. 'Daniel looked desperately ill. His eyes were sunken, his lips cracked and bleeding and although I made him drink a lot he was badly dehydrated,' recalls Victoria. That night their GP rushed him off to King's College Hospital in an ambulance – poor Daniel fainted again as soon as he saw it. At the hospital he fainted and suffered deliriums in turn, and passed blood into a bedpan. Eventually, on a saline and potassium drip, he stabilised. 'He was a pathetic sight.'

At the beginning of the following week it was confirmed that he had been suffering from Salmonella. The whole family, and the school, then had to be tested. They were all in the clear (despite Daniel's rude remarks about his school lunches). Altogether he lost three-quarters of a stone, missed school for five weeks, and was only officially cleared of Salmonella six months later. Since the egg had been completely consumed the cause of his problem has never been finally confirmed. But Daniel and his mother have no doubts. She no longer serves eggs unless they are well cooked, as in Yorkshire pudding or cakes.

Not so long ago Victoria met the Minister of Agriculture at a reception. He told her people were over-reacting about eggs and Salmonella . . . Victoria Bignold told him she did not share his view.

CASE 4: CAMPYLO-WHAT?

Sheila Parker and her unemployed husband John live in Sheffield where they look after their handicapped daughter. In January 1989 Sheila was doing her normal Saturday morning shopping. She bought herself some mussels as a treat for lunch, as well as their usual chicken for Sunday midday. She ate half the mussels at lunchtime with salt and vinegar. Her daughter didn't seem to fancy them so Sheila finished the mussels on Saturday evening.

Sheila roasted the chicken on Sunday, as she does every Sunday and the family enjoyed their lunch. That evening she began to feel ill – sweating and going hot and cold. 'I wasn't sick but I had really bad diarrhoea. This put me in a bit of a panic. You see, I'm 54 and two years before I'd had a heart attack. I thought this might be the start of another one.'

Sheila stayed in bed for three days but still felt no better so she dragged herself to the doctor. The doctor suspected it was Salmonella poisoning but took a test all the same. Meanwhile the outing did Sheila no good at all: 'My knees were like jelly, the diarrhoea came on strongly again and as a result of that I got painful piles.' Piles may be a staple part of music hall humour . . . but they are not funny if you have them.

Three days later the results of the test came through – she

had Campylobacter poisoning. Although this is one of the most common forms of food poisoning few people have heard of it. 'Campylo-what? I said to the doctor,' was Sheila's initial reaction. Then she began thinking about the source. The doctor told her the most common breeding ground for Campylobacter was poultry. But Sheila doubted the chicken was to blame. After all, her husband and daughter had eaten it too and suffered no ill-effects. Whereas she was the only person who had eaten the mussels. But, as in so many of these cases, by the time she went to the doctor there were no leftovers of chicken or mussels and therefore nothing to investigate.

CASE 5: DODGY FOOD

'I worked for Marks and Spencer's 30 years ago and although it's a long time ago I've never forgotten how strong they were on food hygiene. It's imprinted on my mind . . . always throw away dodgy foods.' Lynette McCann is now 61 and lives with her husband John in North London. She is clearly very conscious of the dangers lurking in food, but the problem is that dodgy food does not always give any outward sign of being dangerous.

Lynette made one of her regular visits to her local fishmonger in September 1988 to buy her husband his beloved jellied eels. On this occasion she saw some prawns and, although she rarely eats shellfish, bought some of them for herself. She made a prawn salad and they both enjoyed their lunch very much.

The following morning – Friday – she woke up feeling a little queasy. As the morning progressed she felt worse and worse and diarrhoea set in. She went to see her doctor who diagnosed a stomach bug (she knew that already) and prescribed kaolin and morphine. By Saturday she felt much worse – she was vomiting and had terrible sweats: 'I could cheerfully have gone to hospital.' On Sunday John called out the emergency doctor because she felt so ill and although he reported it to a Health Officer the prawns, of course, were long gone.

For two days the following week she felt better but on the

Wednesday she fell badly ill again. In the end it took three whole weeks for Lynette to recover. She had to forego her cleaning job and the much-needed cash for all that time. She has never eaten prawns again.

CASE 6: SALAD DAYS

John Hauxwell is an architect for the London Borough of Barnet. In July 1988 one of his colleagues was leaving and they all decamped to the local pub to give him a suitably alcoholic send-off. They were not just intending to drink – the pub had a particularly popular buffet where you could have a plate of different salads made up. On that day a rice salad was included on the menu.

John had to return to the office early to conduct a job interview. During the interview the applicant was somewhat thrown by his rapid exit. John suddenly felt extremely nauseous and just managed to get to the lavatory in time. He did not know it then but at that very moment several of his colleagues were also being sick in the pub.

One of the advantages of working for Barnet Council as an architect is that the local Public Health Department is in the same building. Their officials were immediately alerted and with the full co-operation of the pub removed samples of the various salads. John meanwhile sat down at home to watch one of the Wimbledon semi-finals and slept all the way through the match. When he woke up he felt much better and even enjoyed a meal that same evening.

The Public Health officials swiftly found the culprit – the rice salad. It was harbouring Bacillus cereus, often found in rice products. Although it survives boiling, if eaten straight away it causes few problems. But in this case it had been cooked the day before. In addition the pub's fridge had an incorrectly calibrated thermostat so the rice had not been kept cold overnight. The bacterium then formed protective spores which broke open, releasing toxins. Those toxins had hit John's nervous system and caused his illness, thankfully short-lived.

'It must have been very strong to have hit me so hard

because my resistance to bugs is pretty high. I hadn't had a bout of sickness like that for years and had I been the only victim I would never have linked it to food poisoning. I would have put it down to "something not agreeing with me".'

If you would like to know more about how Barnet's Health Department investigated this case you can turn to Chapter 9, page 162.

CASE 7: MALTA FEVER

Rebecca Robertson teaches at a school in Newcastle upon Tyne. This is her experience:

'My husband and I had been spending a week in the Ardèche in a rented villa in August 1987 and were making our way back home through Central France.

'We are keen Francophiles and I have been visiting France regularly since I was a child. One of the many reasons I enjoy it so much is finding off-the-beaten-track restaurants which serve delicious regional food. We stopped for lunch at a nice restaurant in the Auvergne and as I am a piggy eater I couldn't resist trying some of the squidgy-looking local cheeses that Madame la Patronne produced. I tried one locally made goat's cheese as we are always being exhorted by food writers in colour supplements to try the local produce over the more familiar brands you can find at most British supermarkets. I took this advice to heart! My husband is not such a glutton and opted for an ice-cream.

'The following morning I woke up feeling decidedly off-colour, and even more surprising for me – off my food! By the time we arrived in Rheims that afternoon I felt really ill and collapsed into bed. My husband tells me that I was not with it – semi-conscious in fact – and he was terrified in case I fell into a coma. We had a ferry to catch the following day and we were both alarmed by my condition. It felt like a bad case of flu – dizziness, faint and I ached all over. I must have had a high temperature but I didn't have any sickness or diarrhoea. Imagine our delight and surprise when I woke up 12 hours later feeling absolutely fine. It was an extraordinary about-turn'.

'When I got back to school I mentioned the incident to a colleague in the French department. He reckoned I must have had a *fevre de Malte* – Malta fever – which he said is very common in France. The symptoms he described matched mine exactly: "a flu-like illness which could be very serious and nearly always resulted from eating badly made unpasteurised goat's cheese that had become infected." I was quite alarmed and when I looked it up in my dictionary I learnt it was a common name for BRUCELLOSIS – which I'd thought was confined to cattle! My health has always been excellent and I never get any bugs. It's a standing joke in our family. My husband is the one who falls victim to bugs, not me!

'People going across to France for a day trip often have local cheeses at the top of their shopping lists and I think they should be warned of the dangers.' (Interestingly, Rebecca's symptoms were not that unlike a mild attack of Listeriosis.)

CASE 8: I'D NEVER HEARD OF LISTERIA

Angela and Ron Aldred are in their early thirties and they live at Billinge on Merseyside. They had been trying to have a child from the beginning of their marriage and by January 1987, after eight years, Angela was put on a course of fertility drugs. Within six months they were overjoyed to discover she was pregnant. Angela remembers the course of the pregnancy well: 'Apart from the normal morning sickness everything was going fine. Then I started feeling a bit off around the second week in September – this was about 13 or 14 weeks in. But when I went to have an ultrasound scan they told me my baby was fine.'

Because Angela had never had a baby before, she thought the contractions she started having on a Friday not long afterwards were just the effects of her baby moving around. But on Sunday Ron took her to hospital because she was bleeding. The doctors put a stitch in the neck of her womb and put her on a drip to stop the contractions, for that was what she now realised they were. They did all they could for her. But four days later Angela lost the baby she and Ron had longed for.

'I felt totally devastated. We couldn't believe it. I left the hospital the same day because I couldn't bear being around all those mums and babies in the Unit. When I got home I went into seclusion. I couldn't bear to see any of the family except for Ron as I would burst into tears. I didn't go out and I didn't see anyone.'

Fortunately Ron's bosses at the mill where he is a supervising technician were very sympathetic and gave him time off. Meanwhile the doctors carried out a post-mortem, took blood tests and put Angela back on the fertility drug almost immediately. She was delighted to find that she was pregnant again before Christmas.

In mid-January the result of the post-mortem finally came through. It revealed that Angela had contracted Listeriosis. 'I'd never heard of Listeria. Anyway, they gave me a lot of tablets and another stitch in my womb, just to be on the safe side.' In August 1988 Warran was born, weighing 6 lb 11 oz. He was in perfect health 'We went through agony. Our lives were in ruins. Now we have Warran we are thrilled.'

Only after Warran was born did Angela start to read up about Listeria. She discovered that you can catch Listeriosis from soft cheeses. Then she remembered something strange about her first pregnancy. She had developed a craving for soft cheeses. 'I used to buy it all the time . . . Brie, Camembert, anything. Thank God the craving didn't return during my second pregnancy. I'd never have known.'

CASE 9: DAVID PROTHEROUGH

Anna and Mark Protherough's first child, Claire, was coming up for two and in 1985 they decided to have a second child. Mark (a chartered accountant) and Anna were both in their early thirties and felt it was a good time to expand their family.

Anna's second pregnancy was like her first – absolutely normal. So she was surprised, but not unduly alarmed, when she realised that she hadn't felt her baby move for a while. It was mid-August 1986 and five weeks before the birth was expected. 'My first baby had always been very wriggly, especially when I'd been in the bath. But I couldn't feel anything.'

The next morning Anna woke up with contractions and so the hospital near where they live in Hertfordshire told her to come in. She was reassured when they told her they could hear a heartbeat. But the contractions continued and when the doctors detected signs that the baby was in distress they decided to perform an emergency caesarean.

David Protherough was born at 1.30 p.m. and weighed 6 lb. Much to everyone's relief he seemed healthy and normal – so much so that Mark left the hospital for his regular game of tennis. But later in the afternoon David developed breathing difficulties. Then he started having fits – they were starving his brain of oxygen and, it was feared, causing brain damage. Finally he suffered kidney failure as well. By now David had been put on life support machinery and Mark was called back to the hospital urgently. 'When he arrived they asked us whether we wanted David to be christened which meant the worst. I held David in my arms for two hours after we had agreed that the doctors could switch off the support machines. It was extraordinary the way he responded to me – his breathing improved and his colour was much better. So much so that the doctors decided to renew their efforts. Unfortunately, he died soon afterwards.'

David Protherough died before he was one day old. One of the bacteriologists at the hospital had seen a Listeria death two years before and tested for it. Listeriosis was confirmed. When asked, Anna remembered that three weeks before the birth she had felt ill for a day, as though she had flu. But it had soon passed. 'At the time I found just walking to the shops incredibly exhausting which surprised me. But I put it down to the pregnancy.'

Anna soon conceived again and says it was a much more fraught pregnancy. By this time she had seen articles about Listeria. 'I hardly ate any cheese, I didn't go swimming and if my daughter Claire fell over I wouldn't even kiss her directly – anything to avoid picking up a bug.'

John Protherough was born in September 1987 – a healthy 8½ lb baby. Since then Anna and Mark have changed many of their eating habits. They are now very quick to throw anything away which may be near its 'sell-by' date. Anna scrubs the surfaces and chopping boards in the kitchen regularly and shops for food frequently rather than buying large amounts and storing them. 'I think we have all become very lax. We assume all modern foodstuffs are safe. They're not.'

CASE 10: THERE'S SOMETHING WRONG WITH OUR WATER

There are more potential poisons in our food and drink than you would imagine. In the Cornish town of Camelford on the morning of 7 July 1988 Janice Hayne was brushing her teeth before going out. 'My mouth felt as if it was filled with cotton wool – the water tasted foul.' She remembers the date clearly as do many of the residents thereabouts.

Janice Hayne is 45, her husband Jack works in the nearby slate quarry and they live in Camelford with their son Mark. He was seven at the time. Janice dates their current health problems from that fateful day. Jack, who had never had any problems with his digestion, suffered a series of stomach upsets. Eventually his doctor sent him off for a barium meal. This revealed an inflamed duodenum. 'Now he can't eat dairy products and I have to prepare special meals for him,' Janice says.

Janice has been paralysed down her left side since birth. She cannot do anything with her left hand and relies completely on her right. At the best of times it can take her twice as long to do day-to-day things around the house. 'Imagine my horror when I found that my right elbow had seized up with arthritis – I couldn't believe it.' And Mark did not escape . . . he began by developing ulcers in his throat. But then a far more worrying development took place. From being a fairly quiet, well-behaved little boy he became aggressive, often throwing temper tantrums.

Not far away lives Cynthia with her daughter Jennifer. Jennifer, at the age of eight, was a happy child. That July she started to throw tantrums. Cynthia describes it like this: 'Her behaviour was really difficult to take . . . we couldn't say anything without her bursting into tears and yelling at us. It drove us round the bend!'

The local GP, Dr Richard Newman, is an astute man. He noticed that several children coming to his surgery were exhibiting unusually aggressive behaviour. He took samples of their hair, urine and blood and found traces of aluminium. The villagers of Camelford had been poisoned by aluminium.

Eventually the whole story came out. On 6 July 1988 a relief driver had inadvertently tipped 20 tons of aluminium sulphate into the town's reservoir of purified water. He should have tipped it into a storage tank where it would have been used in small quantities in the normal purification process. Most crucially of all, it entered the water supply of 7000 homes in and around Camelford. Only in late February 1989 did the Department of Health finally set about the task of investigating the health of Camelford's residents.

'I feel very angry,' says Janice Hayne. 'The Water Authority have never to my knowledge told us to stop drinking the water except on one occasion before Christmas when they did a flushing-out operation. No one has yet said it definitely *is* the water, but they haven't said it definitely isn't either. It all seems just too much of a coincidence, doesn't it? We are also very worried about the future. We've now heard that aluminium poisoning has been linked to premature senility. How are we going to feel in 10 years' time?'

Now an international flautist – Tim Wheater – is suing the South-West Water Authority for damages. With ulcerated gums, a semi-paralysed lip and general exhaustion he has been unable to work since.

These are 10 incidents of food poisoning – ordinary people who have suffered badly, and sometimes tragically, from something they couldn't control. In some cases they may have been unable to prevent it, however expert they were. In other cases they undoubtedly could have avoided much suffering if they had been taught some of the basic rules of food handling and if someone had explained the risks that ordinary foods can carry with them. Reason enough to learn more?

2 CRISIS? WHAT CRISIS?

All the experts agree that food poisoning is an increasing problem, and a problem that threatens each and every one of us. As we discussed in the Introduction, our food skills have diminished, while modern methods of distribution and cooking have increased the risk of bacteriological poisoning. We now need to recognise the sheer magnitude of the problem. So in this chapter we will take a look at the official statistics, some of them previously unpublished, chiefly because of our obsession with secrecy in this country.

If the thought of statistics fills you with boredom or even horror, do still have a look at them. You will be surprised at how dramatic the rise in food poisoning has been during the last 10 years. Remember that, as in our 'Casebook' in Chapter 1, every single statistic represents ordinary people who have fallen ill, some quite seriously, and a few who have died.

On a day in early February 1989, when it seemed the world and his wife were listening to Edwina Currie give evidence to a parliamentary select committee, a single document was anonymously deposited in the House of Lords' library. In the event, Mrs Currie, whom journalists and MPs had been hounding ever since her resignation over the 'Salmonella in eggs' controversy, said little of interest and absolutely nothing new. The document, on the other hand, was probably the most significant ever to emerge from the vast network of Government ministries and laboratories that concern themselves with public health and the fitness of our food supply. (Even today many of those who run the Government's public health laboratories – where food poisoning statistics are collated and analysed – will not speak to journalists for fear of losing their jobs.)

Luckily for us, while thousands of journalists pursued Mrs Currie through the corridors of power, a rather more independent-minded journalist (*The Times*' political reporter for the House of Lords) spotted the document. For the first time, it tried to give an official estimate of the number of Salmonella poisoning incidents every year in England and Wales. The figure was two million. At last we could look beyond the scare stories in the newspapers and begin to appreciate the scale of the problem. Most cases of Salmonellosis come from food and, after all, Salmonella is only one of several types of bacteria that can give us a 'tummy bug'. (For a better understanding of the different bacteria and the effect they have on us, you can turn to Chapter 9.)

How had officials in the Department of Health and the Ministry of Agriculture hit upon the figure of two million? They had taken the number of confirmed cases of Salmonella in 1987 (20582 to be precise) and multiplied it by 100. Their justification for such a spectacular multiplication was the knowledge that the vast majority of food poisoning cases go unreported and uninvestigated. They never turn up in the official statistics at all. There are several reasons for this:

- If we suffer mild food poisoning for 24 hours with vomiting or diarrhoea we tend to suffer in silence and not go to the doctor. 'It must be something I ate,' we say often enough and then dismiss the incident.
- If the symptoms persist and we go to the doctor the chances are that he will prescribe a simple remedy and advise us to sit it out. Only if our condition does not seem to respond to treatment will he send samples to a hospital or a laboratory for analysis.
- If the tests did confirm a particular form of food poisoning and the Public Health Laboratory was notified we would finally become an official statistic.
- But even if an Environmental Health Officer came to our home to discover the source of the bacteria the likelihood is that we would either have eaten all the offending food in the first place or thrown away what remained. Confirming a case of Salmonella is one thing, establishing its source is quite another.

There has been much debate about whether the number of hidden cases is 100 times greater than the official statistics – or really only 10 times greater. But in the United States experts in this field have used a multiplier of 100 for some time. If those compiling the document hidden in the House of Lords had been working from the figures for 1988 then they would have arrived at around two and a half million (in 1988 the number of Salmonella cases came to just under 25000). And if we look in confidential Government documents we find that the problem is indeed growing year by year. 'Epidemic' is the word the experts are using about the incidence of Salmonella in Britain.

The confidential Communicable Disease Report (CDR) is published weekly by the Department of Health's Public Health Laboratory and contains a constantly updated summary of the national figures. CDR No. 52, covering 1988 and circulated early in 1989, says: 'During the last 12 months the greatest increase in laboratory reports of specific gastro-intestinal infections was seen in Salmonellas.' An accompanying graph illustrates how bad the problem is. And using those figures, we can show how particularly steep the increase has been since 1985.

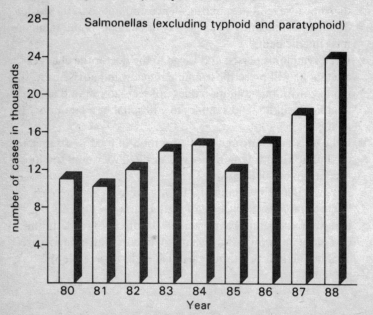

There has been furious debate as to why confirmed cases
of Salmonella poisoning should double over a four-year period.
It is not our task, nor would it help, to become bogged down
here in the argument between poultry breeders and egg pro-
ducers on the one hand, and public health officials on the
other. What is important is to learn how to protect ourselves.
Remember, if the American multiplier is correct this represents
an increase from just over one million to well over two million
between 1985 and 1988.

A further chart from the same Communicable Disease
Report breaks down the recorded incidents for the last three
months of 1988 into types of Salmonella (there are around 2000
strains of Salmonella). Just one of the 2000 strains –
Salmonella enteritidis – accounts for an amazing two-thirds of
the cases recorded between the beginning of October and the
end of December 1988. Salmonella enteritidis, you may not be

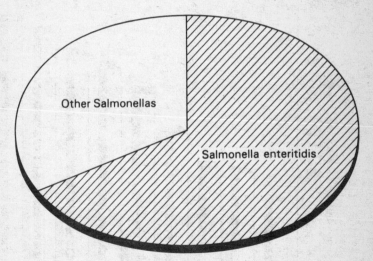

surprised to learn, is particularly associated with poultry. As we
write, the figures for January to March 1989 show a further
escalation – a dramatic increase of 145% over the same period
in 1988.

Much time and energy has been wasted on the controversy
about the safety or otherwise of eggs. Despite the contradictory

statistics, we will never know how many of our eggs have been
contaminated at any given time, whether on the outside of the
shell or deep inside the yoke. But we do know – and this has
been confirmed by the Minister of Agriculture and countless
surveys – that six or seven out of every 10 oven-ready chickens
contain Salmonella. It is not an acceptable figure and it is up
to the poultry industry and the Government to reduce it. We
also know that a particular sort of Salmonella enteritidis –
known as 'phage type 4' – accounts for a sizeable slice of
the current increase and that it is especially associated with
poultry. But Salmonella is only part of the story . . .

The official (but confidential) statistics reveal that one
other bacterium is causing even more illness than Salmonella.
It is called Campylobacter. While the Salmonella controversy
has raged, Campylobacter has quietly attacked an ever greater
number of victims. This is how it has increased this decade.

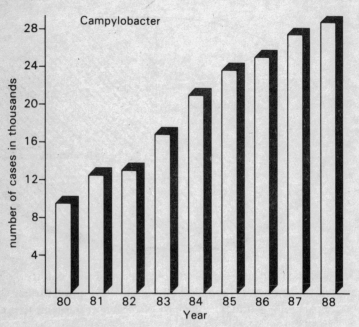

Again, if the American multiplier is correct then those
28 000 confirmed cases in 1988 could really represent almost

three million further victims. No one is suggesting that all Campylobacter and Salmonella poisoning comes from what we eat. (We can pick up bugs from all sorts of places.) But these figures are certainly food for thought.

There is one more bacterium we should briefly talk about. It is far more dangerous than either of the two we have considered so far and, thankfully, poisons us much less frequently – it is Listeria. (For a simple but comprehensive description of what Listeria monocytogenes is and what effect it has on us you can turn to Chapter 9, page 149.) Only someone who is completely isolated from television, radio or the newspapers can have escaped the many Listeria alarms in late 1988 and early 1989. Government scientists, Environmental Health Officers, television programmes and newspapers have all carried out analyses of chilled foods, prepared salads and soft cheeses and found Listeria present in a disturbingly high proportion of the samples.

In 1986 the Government's Food Hygiene Laboratory completed tests on more than 200 soft cheeses. They found Listeria present, sometimes at quite high levels, in 62 cheeses. This they described as 'quite unacceptable'.

Then in January 1989 Environmental Health Officers in Bristol conducted a survey of chilled (not frozen) supermarket foods. They found Listeria in one in 10 pre-cooked chicken meals, and in three out of five raw chicken portions. They also found Listeria in one out of 20 chicken meals prepared for use in local hospitals. (Many of these foods would have been subsequently cooked or reheated, but would it have been for long enough and at a high enough temperature to kill the Listeria, a particularly resilient bacterium?)

At Christmas in 1988 Richard Lacey, Professor of Clinical Microbiology at Leeds University, carried out a survey of convenience supermarket meals for Thames Television's *This Week* programme. He found Listeria in six out of 24 meals. And over a seven-month period Professor Lacey found Listeria in 16 out of 64 meals (13 involving chicken, one in turkey, one in pasta and one in beef spare ribs).

The Government's Food Hygiene Laboratory tested

convenience meals from shops and cook-chill catering units in institutions such as hospitals. They published the results in the medical digest *The Lancet* on 18 February 1989.

PRODUCT	SAMPLES EXAMINED	LISTERIA MONOCYTOGENES DETECTED (IN 25G)
From retail premises		
■ Pre-cooked, ready-to-eat poultry	527	63 (12%)
■ Chilled meals, mainly poultry	74	13 (18%)
From cook-chill catering units		
■ Main course items (prior to reheating)	627	10 (2%)
■ Desserts	73	0

The *Daily Mail* published a further survey of Professor Lacey's on 18 February 1989. He tested 99 soft cheeses (such as Brie and Camembert) bought from 10 supermarkets and 13 small shops. Lacey's team found that one in 11 cheeses contained Listeria, in varying amounts.

It would appear that the soft cheeses contained greater concentrations of Listeria than the convenience foods. On the other hand, convenience meals are far more widely consumed than specialist soft cheeses. At any rate, up to now the official Government statistics on Listeriosis – the illness caused by Listeria – are very small by comparison with the other figures we have looked at:

Cases of Listeriosis in 1987	259
Deaths	23
Deaths (where patient had Listeriosis but may have died from another cause)	59

Note The Department of Health says that in only four of the 23 deaths did the Listeria definitely come from food. Others feel that the problem is much greater than that (see below).

Let's also look, as we have done for Salmonella and Campylobacter, at how Listeriosis has grown in the 1980s. The years 1987 and 1988 saw a considerable growth, from fewer than 150 in 1986 to nearly 300 cases in 1988.

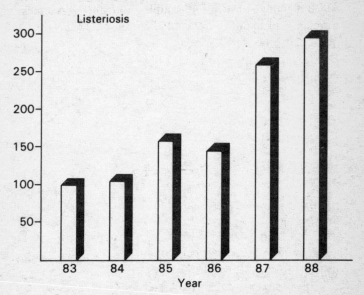

In France the Pasteur Institute estimate that in 1988 they had more than 600 cases of Listeriosis, resulting in around 200 deaths. Despite these higher figures there is less public concern there. But then the French have always taken a rather more robust attitude to their food, and cheese is one of their national treasures. Meanwhile Professor Lacey claims that the number of cases of Listeriosis in Britain – and particularly those that are 'food-borne' – is far higher than the official statistics. He believes that many miscarriages are caused by the bug, for instance.

Listeria is just one more example of official statistics telling only a small part of the story. In fact, as we write, the early results from a large survey by The Food Policy Research Unit at Bradford University have just been released. They suggest (and we can put it no more strongly than that, since the survey results are still being analysed and as yet the sample is small) that in 1988 15 million people had stomach upsets which they attributed to food. The official figure for confirmed cases of food poisoning for the same year is 41 196. We are willing to bet the truth lies rather nearer the first figure.

But enough of such indigestible arguments. It is a massive problem and so much of it could be avoided. That is the whole point of this book.

3 WHAT IS FOOD POISONING?

This chapter describes the common symptoms of food poisoning and its principal causes. With this in mind, you might like to read it *after* your Sunday lunch, especially if you're prone to be a little squeamish about the fauna that live quite happily in and on our bodies. In particular we will be taking a closer look at bacteria. Many of these tiny organisms are essential for our survival, but some can cause severe illness. We will find out just how bacteria like Salmonella, Campylobacter, Listeria and others get into our homes and on to our food.

But what actually is food poisoning? 'Food poisoning' is generally taken to mean any illness caused by eating contaminated or poisonous food. There are many kinds of food contamination, the most common of which is by bacteria, though chemicals, plants, fungi or viruses can have similar effects.

The symptoms of food poisoning are extremely unpleasant, although in healthy adults they rarely last for more than a few days. As we saw in the case studies in Chapter 1, the victim can expect to suffer from vomiting, diarrhoea, abdominal or tummy pain, and fever. In some cases, particularly when the sick, elderly or young are involved, food poisoning can be fatal. The severe dehydration brought on by the vomiting and diarrhoea may cause heart attacks, or the bacteria or poisons simply overwhelm the body's defences causing such a severe illness that the victim cannot cope.

If you have ever experienced food poisoning, and the chances are you have, it might have been some comfort to know that those unpleasant symptoms – vomiting and diarrhoea – are actually part of the body's defence mechanism. Your body recognises that contaminated food has been consumed and if it has only reached as far as your stomach the walls contract and violently squeeze the contents upwards and out of the body. (For further details on the symptoms and treatment of food poisoning you can turn to Chapter 9.)

HOW DO BACTERIA CAUSE ILLNESS?

Symptoms of this kind are usually associated with bacteria that have produced a toxin in the food. A toxin is a poisonous chemical produced by the bacteria, and it is this toxin that irritates the delicate lining of the stomach. If some of the toxin gets past the stomach to the small intestine it may cause an inflammation that is associated with abdominal pain, nausea and diarrhoea.

Other kinds of bacteria are infective, burrowing into the lining of the small and large intestines, and causing infection and inflammation. In very serious circumstances they can even start multiplying in the bloodstream. This type of food poisoning is more commonly associated with diarrhoea and, once again, the symptom can be seen as a defence mechanism. First, water is released into the intestine, tending to wash off the bacteria and lubricate the contents in preparation for rapid removal. Secondly, the muscular contractions that normally push the food along the intestine speed up. The combined effect moves the poisonous or contaminated food very quickly along the intestine and out of the body. The victims find themselves heading very quickly to the loo.

If you're really unlucky, and it's not at all uncommon, you'll get diarrhoea and vomiting at the same time, and serious dehydration can set in. This is why doctors often advise sufferers to drink plenty of liquids.

WHAT DO BACTERIA DO?

Bacteria are essential to life. They are minute single-celled organisms, sometimes referred to as germs, which are everywhere in the environment. They are so tiny that they can only be seen individually with a microscope, although in large numbers they can be observed on laboratory agar plates as colonies (groups of many thousands). On food they can appear as a bacterial slime, for example when 'off' meat is 'sticky' to touch. Have you ever noticed the iridescent 'shimmer' on bacon? That is caused by a harmless bacteria called Pseudomonas.

There are so many bacteria around us, it's quite difficult to imagine their numbers. The vast majority cause no harm whatsoever. It is bacteria that break down compost in a garden compost heap and they that help us digest our food. Indeed, many of them are responsible for the delicious flavours and tastes that we associate with naturally produced products like cheese and yoghurt. Without bacteria the world would be one enormous refuse heap. Nothing would biodegrade and very little, if anything, could survive.

To give you some idea of the numbers of bacteria that one might find in and around a kitchen, take a look at the picture below. That square centimetre on the surface of a tomato could be expected to have as many as 10 000 bacteria on it.

WHERE DO BACTERIA COME FROM?

If bacteria are part of our normal environment, what are the sources of bacteria that can cause food poisoning? Where, for example, do Salmonella come from? Well, it would surprise many people to learn that some of the most common sources of harmful bacteria in their kitchens are the raw foods they buy on a weekly or daily basis. Here are the main danger areas:

Raw poultry and meats

Some animals carry harmful bacteria like Salmonella in their stomachs and intestines. When they are taken for slaughter it is not difficult to imagine how contamination can occur. While the animal is being dressed the slaughterman may accidentally pierce the intestines with his knife, spilling their contents all over the surface of otherwise uncontaminated meat. The contamination is hosed off, and if an Environmental Health Officer sees the incident they will insist the slaughterman sterilises his knife. But let us be realistic. Millions of invisible bacteria will be left on the surface of the meat, starting the long journey to your kitchen and possibly your stomach.

There are strict regulations governing hygiene in slaughterhouses but we have to accept that some contamination is bound to occur. Always consider raw meats, and especially poultry, as potentially contaminated. (For further details on contamination of raw poultry and meat you can turn to Chapter 4, page 65.)

Shellfish

Shellfish, particularly filter feeders like oysters and mussels, are commonly associated with outbreaks of food poisoning. There have recently been some sizeable outbreaks of food poisoning in Britain because our estuaries (where the shellfish are harvested) are contaminated by sewage from coastal towns and cities. Bacteria, viruses and all manner of nasty things may be concentrated in the flesh of some shellfish and if they are not *thoroughly* cooked they can make us very ill. (For further details on contamination of shellfish you can turn to Chapter 4, page 68.)

Unwashed vegetables

Let's not forget that vegetables grow in the soil and it's

obviously impossible, and indeed undesirable, to keep a garden or farm sterile. Farmers use manure and sewage sludge to fertilise their land and to promote growth. So you should always wash vegetables thoroughly. In Canada, for example, in 1981 there was a fairly large outbreak of Listeriosis. It was caused by coleslaw prepared from cabbage grown in a field fertilised by manure from Listeriosis-infected sheep.

Humans

Bacteria are always on and in our bodies. For example it is bacteria that cause septic cuts, spots and boils. This is why good personal hygiene is so important. Approximately 40 per cent of people carry a food poisoning bacteria, Staphylococcus aureus, in their nose and throat. If this is transferred to food via your hands, and allowed to multiply, the bacteria release a chemical toxin that is still dangerous after 30 minutes' boiling.

We can also transfer bacteria from our intestines to food by forgetting to wash our hands after visiting the lavatory. Toilet paper is porous and the germs soak straight through on to your fingers. An unpleasant thought, but nevertheless true. (For further details on personal hygiene you can turn to Chapter 5, page 78.)

Animals

Many animals are an important source for some of the bacteria that can cause disease in man. Pets are no exception and they certainly cannot be expected to follow good rules of personal hygiene! Even a dearly loved dog should not lick our plates and generally should not be allowed in the kitchen too much.

Most people imagine that cats are pretty clean animals. But think how many bacteria they transfer to your work surface as they pad across it after foraging in the neighbourhood dustbins. (For further details on pets you can turn to Chapter 6, page 110.)

Rodents and insects

Rodent and insect pests are filthy creatures carrying harmful bacteria in their gut and certainly on their bodies. They often inhabit sewers and drains, and will feed on anything, including excreta. Their presence in any kitchen environment, whether at home or in commercial premises, is therefore highly undesirable. (For further details on contamination via insects you can turn to Chapter 4, page 74.)

Dirty premises and equipment

We hope everyone recognises that dirty kitchens and equipment harbour bacteria in large numbers. But where exactly? It might be worth having a careful look round your kitchen. Look for dirt traps, especially old equipment, split chopping boards and other nooks and crannies. (For further details on kitchen hygiene you can turn to Chapter 5, page 86.)

WHAT DO BACTERIA NEED?

Now we have covered some of the sources of bacteria in a kitchen, it's worth finding out a little about what they need to grow and develop. Essentially bacteria require four things:

HIGH-RISK FOODS

High-risk foods are foods on which bacteria will readily grow if given the opportunity. They include the following:

- all cooked meat, poultry and meat products, including gravies and stocks
- dairy products, particularly cream, artificial cream, custard and some soft cheeses
- eggs and egg products such as mayonnaise and flans but *excluding* baked items like pastry and some kinds of bread
- rice.

- a food supply
- warmth
- moisture
- and a little time to grow.

Food

Bacteria grow rapidly on the sort of food we particularly like – such as meat, fish and dairy products. Foods with high sugar or salt content are, with one or two exceptions, unsuitable for their growth. This is why jams and salted meats have such a long shelf life.

Warmth

Most of the bacteria that cause food poisoning need warm conditions to multiply and this is very important to remember. Bearing in mind their ability to cause illness in man, it's perhaps not surprising that their favourite temperature is the same as our body temperature (37°C). However they could still multiply at any temperature between 5°C and 63°C – the range

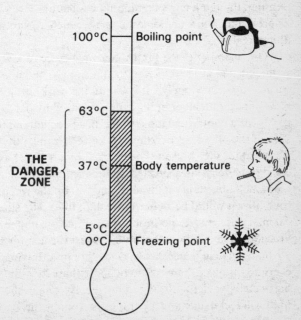

100°C — Boiling point

63°C

THE DANGER ZONE — 37°C — Body temperature

5°C
0°C — Freezing point

often referred to as 'the danger zone'. Most domestic kitchens and centrally heated homes are therefore at the ideal temperature for bacterial growth.

Moisture

Like us, most bacteria need moisture to survive. Unfortunately they don't require very much and therefore most of the foods already mentioned, particularly the high-risk foods, contain more than enough for their growth. However lack of moisture is one of the reasons that dehydrated or dried foods last so long. The bacteria cannot find enough moisture in them to multiply.

Time

Give bacteria the chance and they can multiply to staggering numbers in a very short space of time. They reproduce non-sexually by dividing into two, much like an amoeba. After each cell division the two new cells will divide again, and so on. In ideal conditions (warm and moist) this can happen every 10 minutes, though a more commonly quoted time is 20 minutes. Imagine the following domestic scene which unfortunately is all too realistic.

One member of the family cuts up a piece of raw chicken in the kitchen at 11 o'clock in the morning. The knife is not washed up immediately – it is left on the work surface. At 1 p.m., another member of the family – seized by pangs of hunger – sees a cooked meat pie which has been left out to cool. A slice of the pie is cut with the first knife to hand – the one that was used for the chicken. The chicken blood on it has mostly dried but enough is deposited on the meat pie to leave 100 Salmonella bacteria on the slice and 100 on the rest of the pie (in reality it would be rather more than that). The slice itself, eaten at once, causes no problems. But the pie remains in the warm kitchen all afternoon until the rest is eaten for supper at 7 p.m. Now here is the shocker – by that time, having doubled every 20 minutes, there would be more than 26 million Salmonella bacteria lurking in the pie. No one in the household will feel like eating anything else for a while.

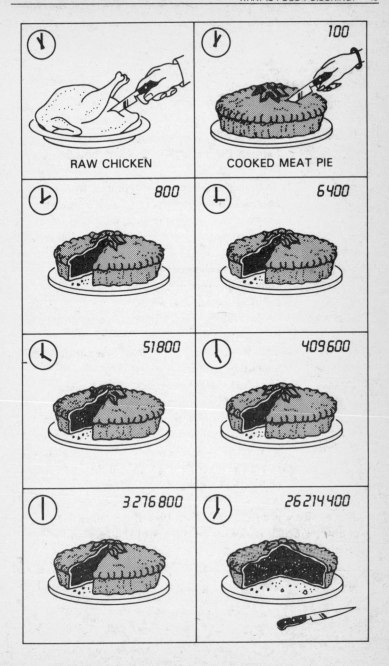

RAW CHICKEN

COOKED MEAT PIE

100

800

6400

51800

409600

3276800

26214400

THE HIT LIST

There have been a number of food scares in the recent past. Here, in a nutshell, is the practical advice currently recommended by the Government and other experts.

Poultry
: Much poultry is contaminated with Salmonella. It should be cooked thoroughly to the bone.

Eggs
: There is a small but proven danger from Salmonella in chicken eggs. No one should eat raw eggs; young children, the elderly, the sick, and pregnant women should avoid semi-cooked eggs.

Soft cheese
: Soft, rinded cheeses such as Brie and Camembert can contain Listeria. They should be avoided by pregnant women.

Chilled food
: Chilled foods, such as pre-cooked TV dinners, may contain Listeria. They should be reheated thoroughly – at least to a uniform temperature of 70°C.

Shellfish
: These are one of the most common causes of stomach upsets, particularly because many British shellfish feed in waters polluted with sewage. Shellfish such as mussels and cockles need to be well boiled to kill off the bugs. In cold weather there's a danger this may not be thorough enough.

This advice was current in March 1989. It may have changed since. If in doubt, consult your local Environmental Health Office.

Viral food poisoning

As we have seen, most outbreaks of diarrhoea and vomiting are associated with the consumption of food that has been contaminated by harmful bacteria. However scientists are now discovering that viruses also cause food poisoning. Investigation of such illnesses is extremely difficult because very few laboratories in Britain, or indeed anywhere, have the facilities to identify the incredibly small viruses. They are much smaller than bacteria and consequently it is only when very large outbreaks come to the Health Authority's attention that they can be investigated in a sufficiently thorough manner to identify viral food poisoning.

The importance of viral food poisoning is increasing. For example, in 1988 more than 10000 reported cases were attributed to viral infection. When such outbreaks have been investigated they have often been associated with our old friends the filter feeders: mussels, cockles and oysters. Unfortunately these really do seem to be fairly risky.

OTHER CAUSES OF FOOD POISONING

Whilst bacteria are undoubtedly the main cause of food poisoning, there are other areas that should be considered.

Chemicals

Chemical food poisoning really falls into two main categories: 'acute poisoning' which basically means something acting quickly if you eat a harmful quantity, and 'chronic poisoning' which involves long-term effects that are often difficult to detect. Most acute poisons are only dangerous when there's a high concentration in food. Some simple examples are the accidental contamination of food or drink with cleaning materials, weedkillers or pesticides. This can occur through carelessness, perhaps when poisonous chemicals are put into unlabelled containers or lemonade bottles, or sometimes through ignorance. Such instances are relatively rare.

In the main, provided you store cleaning agents and other chemicals sensibly, chemical poisoning is not likely to be a problem in the home, unless you have been unlucky enough to purchase a manufactured product that has been contaminated. Many people will recall the dreadful poisoning by contaminated olive oil of some 20000 or more Spanish people between May 1981 and December 1982. At least 350 people died and some are still suffering dreadful illness.

There is mounting concern about pesticide and fungicide residues in fruit and vegetables. What steps can we take at home? We should wash all produce thoroughly (though some treatments are difficult to remove). The other option is to buy organic produce.

Cling film There has recently been widespread concern about cling film (which is found in most homes) and this merits special attention. All packaging 'migrates' into the food it contains in minute quantities. Traditional cling film is moistened and made pliable by an oil known as 'plasticiser'. When this comes into direct contact with oily foods like cheese or fish more than the usual quantity of plasticiser will migrate – though still a minute amount. As a result the Government has advised us for the time being not to use traditional cling film in the volatile conditions of a microwave.

There are now alternative cling films (admittedly less 'clingy') which are free of plasticiser. If you like the qualities of traditional cling film but you don't fancy the idea of 'migration' then use it over the top of a dish, avoiding direct contact with the food. We understand that a Government report expected in late 1989 is likely to give all cling film a relatively clean bill of health.

Metals

Food poisoning can also be caused by metals. David Edwards remembers an interesting case when he was an Environmental Health Officer working in Hemel Hempstead.

'The Environmental Health Department received a complaint from a mother that her young daughter had suffered severe vomiting after eating a can of tinned tomatoes. As is normal in such cases, I immediately went round to interview the mother and daughter.

'When I got to the house I was able to recover the tin can that had contained the tomatoes by digging around in the dustbin (such is the life of a Health Inspector). And it soon became apparent that the young girl had suffered a form of chemical food poisoning from tin and iron which had been dissolved by natural acids in the tomatoes. Most cans used for food are made of tin-plated steel sheet and occasionally, due to prolonged storage or perhaps a canning defect, acid foods such as citrus fruits or tomatoes react with the tin plate. This reaction produces hydrogen gas and also dissolves some of the metal into the food.

'Examining the tin, I could see that the internal lacquering had been eaten away by the acid, and this was what had caused the girl's severe vomiting. She had prepared tomatoes on toast for herself while her mother had been out, and she told me that on opening the can some of the contents had bubbled out of the hole she made, as if under pressure. This was exactly what one would expect if the can was 'blown', meaning that gas had formed inside as a result of the acid attack on the surface.

'Subsequent laboratory examination confirmed very high levels of metal contamination in the remaining tomatoes. And a visit to the local corner shop revealed a few other cans at the back of the shelves which had been there since the dawn of time. A careless shop owner, a young girl who knew no better, and the result was an unfortunate and extremely unpleasant experience.'

This is one reason why people are always advised to empty any can of food into another container once it's been opened. The presence of oxygen accelerates the chemical attack on the surface of the tin. You can observe this for yourself if you leave a half-empty can of tomatoes in the fridge for a couple of days. When you remove the remaining tomatoes you will see a tidemark, showing how the internal surfaces of the can have been attacked by the high level of acid. It's not an experiment I would recommend if you want to eat the food!

There are several other metals which can cause food poisoning; the symptoms would normally be vomiting and abdominal pain although much more serious long-term effects can sometimes occur. One of the ways in which poisonous metals can come into contact with food and cause harm is via utensils, pots, pans and containers. Equipment manufactured by reputable companies in the developed world is unlikely to cause such problems, but if you buy earthenware or cooking equipment from other more exotic countries you should be very careful about using it in your kitchen. The following metals can be found in pans, utensils and other kitchen equipment.

Aluminium There has been much concern in 1988 and 1989 about aluminium in the food supply and its effect on our bodies. It is suspected by some doctors – but not yet proven – that intake of relatively high amounts of aluminium over a long period of time can cause premature senility (Alzheimer's Disease). There have been worries about the levels of aluminium in some baby foods, particularly those given to very young babies. Indeed, three experts gave the advice recently (*The Lancet*, 3 March 1989) that mothers should give their infants soya milk only on doctor's advice. They feared that the relatively high levels of aluminium in soya milk (usually prescribed when a baby is intolerant of cow milk in the first few weeks of life) added to water that may also be relatively high in aluminium could hurt the baby's system – particularly in the long term. *If you are concerned about this you should consult your doctor who will advise you.*

But a number of *Food and Drink* viewers, reacting to the suggested link with Alzheimer's Disease, wrote to ask whether they should be using aluminium saucepans or foil. The short answer is that there is no hard evidence that aluminium saucepans or foil represent a danger. However, there is an interesting piece of food chemistry involved here.

As we have said, all food packages and containers absorb minute quantities of the food they contain, *and vice versa.* The amount depends on the materials involved. Aluminium is particularly sensitive to acid. If you cook a highly acidic food like rhubarb in an aluminium saucepan then more aluminium leaches out into the food than happens with other more neutral foods. There is now some evidence that water supplies which have had fluoride added intensify this process. Likewise, if you store pizzas with tomato topping (which is highly acidic) in aluminium foil for long enough the acid eats holes in it.

Few people are suggesting we should give up using aluminium saucepans and foil altogether. Indeed where saucepans are concerned, non-stick surfaces create a barrier (until they wear away). Where foil is concerned, packaging manufacturers have developed 'barrier-coated' foils specifically for acidic foodstuffs. But if this migration of aluminium worries you then avoid using aluminium materials with highly acidic foods like fruit and vegetables. If you have been making jams and chutneys in aluminium preserving pans and you wish to change we recommend stainless steel replacements (though we should warn you they are rather more expensive).

And watch out for aluminium coffee pots, too. A US survey published in *The Lancet* in April 1989 showed that tap water boiled in such a pot had thirty times the recommended aluminium limits in it.

Copper is commonly used for cooking utensils and it can be attacked by acid foods. It would not usually cause a problem in your kitchen because the acid food or drink would be only briefly in contact with the copper. (It takes quite a long time for copper to leach in quantities large enough to cause illness.) However the danger occurs when making chutneys and the like. Copper saucepans should not be used for such purposes as the vinegar will react chemically with the copper to produce copper salts that could poison you.

Lead is a very poisonous substance and has been in the news a great deal recently because of the campaign to remove it from petrol. It is capable of causing both acute and chronic poisoning. Earthenware containers are sometimes glazed with lead oxide compounds and so acid products should not be stored in them. There is no doubt that the less we expose ourselves to lead and lead compounds the better. Some of the more reputable supermarkets warn that when you remove the lead foil around some wine bottles you should wipe the glass surface clean with a soft damp cloth. This is always good practice.

Cadmium is used quite extensively for plating utensils and containers and is readily attacked by acid foods and wines. Earthenware containers made in some countries have been known to contain acid-extractable cadmium and again should not be used to store acid products.

Antimony is a metallic element used in some enamels. If you are not sure of the origin of any enamelled equipment do not use it, especially with high-acid foods.

Poisonous plants and fungi

Poisonous plants seldom cause food poisoning in restaurants but have been known to cause problems at home when people have eaten poisonous mushrooms by mistake. Even some common vegetables have poisonous parts. For example, tomato and potato plants belong to the same family as deadly nightshade and all green parts of these plants contain a chemical poison called solanine. Potatoes are not poisonous as long as they are kept underground or stored in the dark, but if exposed to light they start to turn green and become poisonous. Fortunately they taste bitter and unpleasant, and few cases of such poisoning occur.

Rhubarb is another common vegetable that can be poisonous. The leaves contain a poison called oxalic acid and there have been cases of food poisoning when they have been cooked and eaten as a form of spinach. Fortunately there is very little of the oxalic acid poison in the stalks and we can eat those quite safely.

Red kidney beans

From 1976 outbreaks of poisoning have been reported in Britain by people who have eaten red kidney beans which have been cooked incorrectly. In fact between 1976 and 1982 there have been 26 reported incidents of food poisoning affecting over 118 people. A naturally occurring poison is responsible for the illness, which can be quite severe. Symptoms develop soon after eating the beans and have also been associated with the use of slow-cook ovens which do not reach sufficiently high temperatures to destroy the poison. Investigations into the outbreaks show that as few as four or five beans are enough to cause symptoms of food poisoning if they have not been properly cooked. The poison can be destroyed by *boiling for 10 or more minutes.*

The outbreaks of kidney bean poisoning actually received a fair amount of publicity, even reaching national television, and the Department of Health subsequently asked the grocery trade to place advisory labels on raw beans. (You have probably noticed them in supermarkets.) But our advice is to buy tinned kidney beans. All canned foods receive very effective heat treatment which is more than enough to ensure that the beans are safe.

Poisonous fish

Fish is a very healthy food and a good source of protein. It is less commonly associated with bacterial food poisoning because its environment, the sea, is generally very cold; the bacteria that live on fish do not usually like the warmer temperatures of our bodies and are therefore less inclined to attack us. Nevertheless, common food poisoning bacteria like Salmonella will grow readily on fish and fish products. It is just that they are unlikely to be found there in the first place.

Some unusual fish *are* actually poisonous. Perhaps the most infamous example of this is a particular Japanese delicacy – the 'Fugu' fish. Many restaurants in Japan employ specially trained chefs who are capable of preparing this particular fish. This is because certain parts, especially its liver and sex organs, are exceptionally poisonous. Unless these are completely removed you are likely to suffer severe food poisoning, with a 60 to 70 per cent chance of death. Apparently Japanese gourmets relish not only the slight tingling sensation of the palate from the remains of the toxin in other parts of the fish, but also the thrill of eating a meal that could well be their last if the chef has had a bad day!

In 1975 a Japanese restaurant in London began to offer Fugu fish prepared by an expert chef but City of London Environmental Health Officers and the Fish Inspectors at Billingsgate Market combined their not inconsiderable force and persuaded a magistrate to condemn the fish as unfit for human consumption.

There is one other type of fish poisoning that occurs occasionally. It is called 'scombrotoxic fish poisoning' and there are a number of outbreaks in most years. The precise mechanism by which the poisoning occurs is quite complex but the illness appears to be very similar to an allergic food poisoning. The toxin involved resembles histamine (the chemical released by the body during allergic reactions). Certainly histamine alone, or in combination, is thought to be responsible for the illness. And histamine has been found at high levels in fish suspected of causing this type of food poisoning.

These are usually 'oily' fish, particularly mackerel, but also tuna, sardines and pilchards. The toxin seems to form in such fish when they have been incorrectly stored (for instance, left in a warm room instead of being refrigerated). Even when canned these oily fish can cause problems because once formed, the toxin is extremely heat-resistant and will not be destroyed by normal processing.

KEEPING A SENSE OF PERSPECTIVE

Bacteria, viruses, toxins, chemicals in food, poisonous fish – it all seems a sorry tale and you might reasonably ask yourself, why are we not dying in our thousands? Is anything safe to eat and is this not just a bit of an over-reaction?

Well, you would certainly be right to try and put the problem into perspective. Very many more people die as a result of road accidents, and the nation's health is much more severely affected by cigarettes, alcohol, unhealthy eating and poor diet than the problems of food poisoning. However it is a cause for concern that food poisoning is rising dramatically and we seem to have a poor record compared with our European neighbours and indeed many other parts of the world.

Furthermore, over the last 15 to 20 years, the average consumer has been lulled into a false sense of security. Food is neatly packaged and attractively displayed in the bright hygienic-looking surroundings of modern supermarkets. When buying food on our weekly shopping expeditions it is hard to believe that some of it could make us extremely ill, or even kill us. It seems such an unreasonable and paranoid thought that most of us dismiss the idea and rely on the supermarkets and manufacturers to keep us safe. Unfortunately recent events have shown that this really isn't a sensible option and following some simple rules can greatly reduce our chances of being poisoned by the food we buy (see Chapters 4 and 5).

Having said all this, one needs to maintain a healthy scepticism. There's nothing some newspapers enjoy more than a story which gives us dire warnings that we are all about to be poisoned. Perhaps this is occasionally true. If you have put yourself on an uninterrupted diet of uncooked shellfish, have a craving for tinned food in a can opened three days ago, eat large quantities of jam boiled up in an aluminium pan, or consume chicken steamed in cling film every day . . . then perhaps you should modify your habits. Otherwise you probably have little to worry about.

FOOD SPOILAGE

For the sake of clarity, we need to distinguish between food spoilage and food poisoning. We all know that food is perishable and poor or prolonged storage can cause changes that make it unpleasant to eat.

The changes that come under the heading 'food spoilage' include surface slime, unpleasant smells or an alteration in odour, flavour or texture. Sometimes they are caused by chemical changes in the food – for instance the fats may oxidise and become rancid. Or they may be the result of bacterial action which is the case when milk goes 'off' or mould grows on jam.

Food spoilage makes the food unpleasant and even impossible to eat but it does not necessarily make it harmful.

Interestingly enough, in some circumstances food spoilage bacteria may actually help prevent food poisoning. As spoilage bacteria are not harmful they can perform a useful 'indicator' function by warning us that food is old or has been kept at the wrong temperature. They also compete with harmful bacteria for food and moisture, thus providing a useful natural control.

Some would argue that this is an argument for restricting irradiation of food because it kills off harmful bacteria but also kills off spoilage bacteria and other indicator organisms. If the food is subsequently recontaminated with harmful bacteria, like Salmonella, they have free range and can multiply to their hearts' content. Furthermore, none of the spoilage bacteria are present to warn us that the food is unfit to eat.

It all goes to show how complex the whole issue of food safety is, and why it is so important that decisions about our food are made by people who are totally unaffected by any commercial interests. Though the broader questions may be complex, as we have said before, there are some simple guidelines we can all follow to keep ourselves and our families healthy. The next two chapters give practical advice on buying, storing, preparing and cooking food safely.

4 SHOPPING AND STORING

We have now looked at the various types of food poisoning and concluded, with a couple of exceptions, that bacterial contamination is the main culprit. The Government's own estimates suggest that a minimum of two million people suffer the effects of food poisoning every year and others put it much higher. A high proportion (perhaps as many as half of these) are thought to occur in small family outbreaks.

However food poisoning is avoidable and simple rules, sensibly applied, can virtually eliminate it from the home. A basic understanding of the needs and habits of bacteria will help us identify these precautions. They are as effective in the home as they are in any modern food factory, restaurant or supermarket.

Serving safe food starts with choosing and buying the raw ingredients or, more commonly these days, partially or completely prepared convenience items. In order to shop safely you need to be able to judge whether the shops you use are operating at sufficiently high standards. In business, good hygiene is primarily about good management. The technical skills required to handle food correctly are relatively straightforward. The difficulty for people running food businesses is ensuring that their staff follow the rules, and that comes down to good management. Poor or indifferent managers will either be ignorant of the proper standards or, worse still, unconcerned if they drop below an acceptable level.

BUYING GROCERIES

The grocery trade in Britain has been revolutionised since the war. Most people now shop once a week at one or more of the well-known supermarkets (we now buy more than half our groceries from just six companies). Since 1961 well over 100 000 grocer's shops (three-quarters of the then total) have closed. And ever larger supermarkets continue to be built on out-of-town sites.

To help you judge the quality of your shop – whether on the corner or a supermarket – here are some areas where standards slip.

Chillers and freezers

Display cabinets in supermarkets and shops often have red 'load lines' marked on the inside of the cabinet. If food is stored outside these load lines it starts to warm up, reducing its keeping quality and possibly allowing growth of harmful bacteria like Listeria.

Shops, particularly supermarkets, are sometimes under pressure to move stock very quickly. For this reason they may turn a blind eye to their staff overloading chillers or freezers and piling food above the load line. Of course, for them, it is far less work than continually refilling the shelves, but you should always avoid any food which has not been stored correctly. This, incidentally, is something we could all tackle by complaining to the manager if we see it.

Refrigeration temperatures

Low temperatures are vital if bacterial growth is to be controlled and some recent surveys by Environmental Health Departments have shown up problems, particularly with the open shelving used in most supermarkets. Although these surveys have been quite small, they may well reflect a national picture. If this is the case, the industry has a real problem because providing more efficient refrigeration would be very costly for supermarket chains that have old or inefficient models in their stores.

As a consumer, you can check that those display chillers and freezers which have visible temperature dials are working at the correct temperatures. For chilled food, this should be up to $3°C$ and for frozen food $-18°C$ or below.

Another sign of poor temperature control is when frozen foods such as peas or beans are in solid lumps in their packets.

These products are individually 'quick-frozen', which means they should be loose in the packet. If they are clumped together it means they have been partially thawed and have re-frozen together in a lump. This indicates bad practice and a break in the 'cold chain' that supermarkets and shops should maintain.

Cans and packaged goods

In principle the sale of dented cans and broken packaged goods is not a problem. It allows people to buy quality foods at low cost. However there are some dangers if the practice is not properly controlled. Unfortunately it is not uncommon to find canned goods on sale that are severely dented on the seam or rim. Such cans should have been sorted out and disposed of because the seam damage can allow invisible cracks to form, letting air or bacteria, or both, into the contents. With high-acid foods, like tomatoes and some fruits, this could cause the illness described in Chapter 3, page 53. In short, *don't* buy cans that are dented on the seam or rim. Ask the manager to remove them from sale.

Dry goods, such as breakfast cereals, are normally all right if just the external packaging is damaged. However take a closer look at any inner wrappings (to make sure that they are undamaged) before you buy. It is also worth checking the 'sell-by' or 'eat-by' dates.

To some extent, the large supermarket chains like Tesco and Sainsbury's have led the field in improving standards of retail hygiene, although many people in the industry would give Marks & Spencer the highest accolade. These companies have all employed teams of Environmental Health Officers and Food Technologists for many years to assess standards of hygiene, both in their own stores and also at the premises of their suppliers and distributors. However the rapid growth of the supermarket business, with thousands of individual food lines on sale in any one shop, has strained distribution systems to the limit. Supermarkets remain one of the best places to buy good-quality, hygienically prepared food. But as consumers we must keep up the pressure for high standards.

Cleanliness

The overall standard of cleanliness in any supermarket or shop is a good guide to the attitude of the management to food safety. If something as obviously noticeable as cleanliness is lacking then it is reasonable to assume that other more important aspects, like temperature control, will also be badly managed.

In supermarkets and shops, dirty shelving, dirty floors and dirty display cabinets are all things to look out for. A commonsense judgement is as good a guide as any in this situation. Just stop for a moment, look around you, and decide whether you think the shop is really clean.

Staff hygiene

You may be surprised to learn that anyone running a food business (whether it is a restaurant, shop, or supermarket) need have no training in food hygiene whatsoever. If you know what to look for, you'll soon be able to tell whether the people serving you have had any training. Staff behind a serving counter should always exhibit the best personal hygiene standards and the information box lists some of the signs to look for.

RECOGNISING STAFF HYGIENE

- Staff should be wearing clean overalls or uniforms and should not wipe their hands on their clothing. If they have dirty hands they should wash them in a nearby hand basin.
- Staff should not touch their hair or face while serving customers.
- Hair should be tied back and preferably be completely enclosed by a clean head covering or hairnet.
- Hands should be clean with short, clean fingernails and no nail varnish or jewellery.
- Cuts or abrasions of the skin, especially on the hands, should be covered with a coloured (usually blue) waterproof plaster.

The corner shop

Although the number of small retail grocers has contracted
considerably most people still have a corner shop nearby that
can compete with the supermarket, perhaps not on price but
certainly on convenience. And many provide an excellent service. However (at the risk of offending those small shops that do
maintain very good standards) you would be wise to be a little
more careful when buying foods from shops where the level of
hygiene depends almost entirely on the attitude and knowledge
of an individual owner. Small businesses find it difficult to
invest in training and some owners have little idea of the
proper standards. Running the local shop and Post Office may
be a long-cherished dream for many people, but the practical
reality is that margins are tight and there is a temptation – or
perhaps sometimes a necessity – to cut corners.

BUYING MEAT AND POULTRY

The British are still a nation of meat eaters
and although there is a definite trend
towards the leaner cuts of red meat, and
towards white meat (like chicken) a trip to
the butcher's is still a regular event for most
shoppers. There are just as many hygiene
problems to look out for when you go to
the butcher's as at the grocer's.

Displaying meat

Over the past few years you may have noticed some butchers
displaying meat products outside their shops on tables that are
often unrefrigerated. Even in winter, particularly our recent
mild ones, this is bad practice. You would be well advised to
avoid shops which place perishable food outside in such an
exposed situation. Surprisingly, the law does not prohibit this
but any Environmental Health Officer worth his or her salt
should be able to apply enough pressure to the shop owner to
stop the practice. If you see it in your high street you could
report it to your local Environmental Health Officer.

While we are on this subject, displaying cooked meats like ham joints in the traditional manner (on a porcelain pedestal at the back of the shop) is totally unsatisfactory. Remember that ham is a product that some bacteria can grow readily upon, and it is not going to receive any further cooking. It should be chilled.

Raw and cooked meat

Another area where butchers sometimes fall down is the prevention of cross-contamination from raw to cooked food.

RECOGNISING QUALITY IN MEAT

- *Beef* tissue should be pink to red and flecked with fat to give a marbled appearance. The fat should be creamy-white, brittle and firm. Some beef, fed on a particular diet, will have a slightly more yellowish fat. Well-hung beef will be dark red.
- *Lamb* should be bright red, firm to the touch and have white, brittle and flaky fat.
- *Pork* should be pale pink and firm, and the fat should be white and hard.
- *Offal*, like meat, should never have an unpleasant, 'off' odour.
- *All these meats* should smell fresh and be free of any stickiness (which is due to bacterial growth and decomposition).
- *Chicken* should have firm, glossy white flesh and unbroken skin that is free of any bruising or blood spots. The scales on the legs should be smooth and there should be no unpleasant smell or discoloration of the flesh. Some birds have a yellow tinge to the fat, caused by the feed, and this is no problem. One other tip is that young roasting birds should have a pliable tip at the base of their breast bone. If this bone is firm and hard it has ossified, suggesting the bird has reached a ripe old age. You have been ripped off.

A qualified butcher does receive basic hygiene training but many seem to have become so used to handling raw meats that they forget how important it is to keep them completely separate from cooked meats. It's very important that they have a separate set of scales and complete separation of cooked and raw foods in their display cabinets. They should also be careful to wash their hands between handling cooked and raw food.

How safe is meat?

All meat and offal is inspected by qualified Environmental Health Officers or Meat Inspectors at a slaughterhouse. They will usually have removed any meat that has been affected by cysts, liver flukes or other harmful organisms and conditions. Nevertheless, it is impossible to have a 100 per cent reliable inspection regime, and diseased meat and offal can sometimes get through the system. It is very rare but if you see anything you're not sure about, ask your local Environmental Health Officer.

Sawdust

Something else you may have noticed in many butchers is that sawdust is spread on the floor to prevent staff slipping over. These days sawdust can be replaced with other compounds that are chemically inert, and less likely to accidentally contaminate meat. Sawdust is unhygienic.

BUYING FISH

Generally speaking, fish is not only a very healthy food, it is also safe in terms of microbiological hazards. As already mentioned, their normal environment is cold. The bacteria that grow on fish find our warm body temperature unacceptable and are therefore less likely to affect human beings. However, unlike meat and game, fish does not improve with age (though 12 hours can help relax the muscles). It can go off very quickly so it must be purchased while fresh. To make a judgement about fish, we can simply use our senses – sight, smell and touch.

RECOGNISING QUALITY IN FISH

- *Colour* should be bright and clear.
- *Skin* should have a shiny, glistening appearance.
- *Eyes* should be bulging and prominent with a clear black centre and not opaque or misty.
- *Gills* should be pink to red in colour and free of any slime. If smelt, the gills should have a pleasant seaweedy odour.
- *Scales* should be firm and not readily rubbed off.
- *Odour* should be fresh with no trace of unpleasantness or ammonia.
- *Texture* should be stiff and rigid, not floppy and loose.
- *Fish fillets* should be firm and elastic and not crumble under finger pressure. They should not have an unpleasant or ammonia odour.

SHELLFISH

In Chapter 3, we referred to shellfish as a major cause of viral food poisoning. 'Filter feeders', including oysters, cockles and mussels, are known to concentrate viruses from sewage-polluted water, so shellfish grown in such water must be regarded with suspicion. Unfortunately it seems that many British coastal and estuarine waters are now sewage-polluted. For some reason the problems with shellfish have not hit headlines to the same extent as those involving cheese, eggs and chilled meals, but they should certainly take their place with these foods as yet another example of our failure to keep our food chain safe.

Back in 1986 the Food Hygiene Bureau became aware that such incidents with shellfish were increasing. Conversations

with representatives of the Department of Health revealed a
national problem. In May the Bureau wrote a very specific letter to its commercial catering clients strongly advising them not
to use filter-feeding shellfish from British waters. Certain
suppliers were harvesting shellfish from waters heavily contaminated with sewage and the danger was compounded by
unusually cold seas. When the shellfish were then boiled for
the normal length of time they did not reach a sufficiently high
temperature to kill off the bugs. Other cleansing procedures
and storage in acetic acid would not necessarily have made the
shellfish safe. *The Bureau has not withdrawn this advice.*

The Communicable Disease Surveillance Centre state in a
1987 report: 'the association of gastro-enteritis viruses with bi-
valve molluscs suggests unacceptable levels of sewage contamination of the estuarine waters from which these shellfish are
harvested'. Later they say: 'in the light of recent reports, it is
clear that bi-valve molluscan shellfish, particularly cockles and
oysters, cannot be supplied with a guarantee that they are free
of virus contamination and therefore continue to pose a risk to
public health if eaten raw or without adequate cooking.'

Surely such a situation is not acceptable. It is a disgrace
that clients of the Food Hygiene Bureau had to be advised to
buy shellfish from other countries. It cannot be right that major
outbreaks of food poisoning are avoided only if we have warm
winters when the heat treatment of shellfish is more effective.
Furthermore, we are not just talking about simple food poisoning and 'a dose of the trots'. The same report refers to a suggestion that as many as 18000 reported cases of infectious jaun-
dice during the period 1979 to 1983 may have been Hepatitis A
caused by shellfish or by other foods. The evidence for such an
assertion is circumstantial but is nonetheless cause for concern.

Hepatitis is a serious condition and it is hard to understand why the problem has not received greater coverage.
Meanwhile sewage pollution remains a serious problem in
many of our coastal waters.

Our advice is to eat filter feeding shellfish only when they
have been *thoroughly cooked.*

TRANSPORTING FOOD

Having bought your food, you now need to get it home safely. Perishable foods, particularly chilled or frozen items, should be taken home as quickly as possible and put in your own refrigerator or freezer. It is possible to buy large insulated bags for frozen and chilled foods. These are obviously a good idea, particularly in the summer months, when the boot of your car warms up very quickly.

If you keep the chilled and frozen foods together in a solid mass they warm up less quickly, but *don't* do this if the packaging is leaky. This is where you need to watch out for accidental cross-contamination from raw to cooked foods. And that's why many supermarkets double-wrap raw meats to prevent them leaking on to other cooked items in the same shopping bag.

Another problem that can occasionally occur when transporting food in the car is accidental contamination by chemicals, anti-freeze or other strong-smelling items that may also be in the boot.

STORING FOOD

The 'shelf life' of food is a guide to how long an item remains in peak condition under ideal storage conditions. Of course a variety of chemical and bacteriological changes take place in all foods over a period of time, and many such changes are welcome. For example meat is always 'hung' for a few days to allow it to tenderise and improve its flavour. Many people also prefer soft cheeses like Camembert to 'mature' a little, until the texture is soft and runny with a strong and characteristic flavour.

Nowadays, many perishable foods are required to have a 'best-before' date. However you will sometimes also see 'sell-by' and 'eat-by' dates. It is very confusing and there needs to be some revision of the law to make the advice more consistent.

Many foods can still be purchased loose, and are not pre-packed, so how do you tell what the shelf life is in such circumstances? The information box gives some guidelines, but remember to examine the food before you cook or eat it. As usual, a commonsense judgement is probably as good a guide as any. The following shelf lives depend on so many other factors, like the efficiency of your refrigerator, or how the food was handled in the shop. For these reasons, they can only give a rough indication.

RECOMMENDED STORAGE TIMES

TYPE OF FOOD	DAYS IN THE REFRIGERATOR	MONTHS IN THE FREEZER
Raw meats		
Beef	4	6–9
Pork	4	6–9
Lamb	4	6–9
Mince	1–2	3
Sausages	3	3
Poultry	2	9
Bacon	7	1
Cooked meats		
Ham	2–3	3
Pâté	2–3	1
Poultry	2–3	1–2
Fish		
White fish	1–2	6
Shellfish	1	3
Dairy products		
Milk (pasteurised)	3–4	
Cream	2–3	
Eggs	6–8	

Storage in the refrigerator

The correct storage of food in a refrigerator is a pretty straight-forward affair. We've already discussed the importance of low temperatures in controlling bacterial growth. So the first job on returning from the shops is to refrigerate all the perishable and chilled foods as soon as possible. Here are a few tips on the safest way of loading your fridge:

- Unpack perishable and chilled foods first and load the refrigerator in one go.
- If you need to rearrange items remember that it's vitally important to keep raw and cooked foods separate. An overcrowded or badly organised refrigerator is where they most commonly come into contact, leading to possible cross-contamination.
- Remember the importance of air circulation if your fridge is to work correctly. If you find yourself packing things in untidily and on top of one another, then it's pretty likely you've overloaded the fridge, preventing the air from circulating.
- Make sure all food containers that you put in the refrigerator are clean.
- Don't let stale food accumulate – check your fridge frequently.
- Most foods should be covered, either with cling film or aluminium foil. This helps prevent cross-contamination and also stops food drying out. (But see our notes on cling film, Chapter 3, page 52; and aluminium, Chapter 3, page 54.)

If you give a party and have an unusual amount of food that needs refrigerating it may be advisable to turn the temperature of the fridge down an hour or two before you put the extra food in. This allows it to cope with the extra load. *Never* put hot food in the fridge as the domestic type cannot cope properly with such demands.

It's not unusual for some items, particularly cheese and vegetables, to develop mould growth in refrigerators. Most moulds are not harmful, although some are. You can safely trim cheese but be sure to cut away at least half an inch of any mouldy surface. Other mouldy foods, particularly vegetables, should be thrown away immediately before they affect other items stored with them.

Of course all these precautions are pointless if your fridge is not at the correct temperature to start off with. A refrigerator thermometer is therefore a useful tool. (For further details on fridge and freezer thermometers you can turn to Chapter 7, page 125.)

Storage in the freezer

Frozen food should be put away as quickly as possible. You do have a little more time as it is normally kept at −18°C or below, and dense items, like meat, will not rise significantly in temperature over a short period of time. However, less dense foods (like peas, beans and chips) do start to defrost quite quickly and although there is little hygiene risk (as these are low-risk foods) some quality will be lost.

Home freezing is much slower than its commercial equivalent, and large ice crystals form in the food, breaking its substance up. This is why delicate items like strawberries do not freeze well.

It's generally a good idea to wrap the various items in freezer bags or containers and label them with purchase or home freezing dates. As you'll be keeping the food for quite a long time, perhaps several months, it will be very difficult to remember when you purchased or froze it. The freezing process can also dry out foods. This is known as 'freezer burn' and can be prevented by covering the food.

Neither the freezer nor the fridge should be kept in a small room as the heat exchangers at the back require good air circulation. Hot air rising from the heat exchanger will also warm up your cupboards and any dry goods will perish more quickly at warmer temperatures.

Tinned and bottled food

Tinned food will keep for a very long time because the manufacturing process sterilises the product. The main exception to this rule is tinned ham which is usually only pasteurised and must be kept in a refrigerator both before and after opening. (For further details on storage of tinned food, once the can has been opened, you can turn to Chapter 3, page 53.)

Bottled foods, like some tomato ketchups made without preservatives, can ferment and explode if they are not kept refrigerated (as Sainsbury's found to their cost when the *Sun* featured their 'exploding ketchup'). Read the label so as to keep a close eye on the ingredients. If there are no preservatives don't leave it in a warm room. Jams and chutneys can sometimes develop mould. If in doubt it is probably safer to throw the whole lot away. It is hard to tell how far the mould has spread in such foods and as some moulds are harmful it's better not to take the risk.

Storage in the larder

Until fairly recently, building regulations used to stipulate that kitchens had to be provided with ventilated food cupboards. It's a pity that this particular requirement is no longer considered necessary, as a cool dry place for dry goods is still useful even in today's high-tech kitchen.

Food safety in the larder really depends on two things:
- good stock rotation
- and preventing pest infestations.

The easy way to ensure that dry goods such as gravy powder don't stay in the cupboard for years on end is to keep your oldest stock at the front of shelves and the newest stock at the back. That way, you use up the oldest items first. This system is used by all good shops and supermarkets and works just as well at home.

Dealing with pest infestations is slightly trickier and certainly a job for the experts if you have anything more than a minor problem. It's not uncommon for homes to be infested by mice or insects, and your best method of control is probably just to keep the cupboards clean. Pests are likely to be attracted to scraps of food left around in an untidy cupboard.

Here are a few tips on storing food safely in your larder:
- Air-tight containers are best for flour and similar dry goods.
- Clean up any spillages as quickly as possible, otherwise they will attract insects.
- Rotate stock – oldest at the front of the shelves and newest at

- Keep cupboards dry and clean.
- Look out for signs of infestation. Droppings and gnawed packets are both clues. Take expert advice if you do have an infestation.

If you have any insects in your store cupboard, you should collect a couple of samples and take them for identification to your local Environmental Health Department. For any

COMMON PESTS

There are many pests that can infest stored food but here are a few of the more common ones:

Ants	Ants' nests are situated outside but they forage for food inside. They are mostly just a nuisance but food they have come into contact with should be thrown away. Ant poison should then be placed in or near the nest.
Psocids	These are tiny grey or brown insects which like warmth, humidity and dark crevices. In other words, a food packet in the average kitchen is ideal. If they appear, you can kill them by spraying the cupboard with fly spray. All packets – open or shut – should be thrown away first. Sealed bottles and tins can be kept but paper labels should be soaked off under the tap. If you have suffered from psocids the chances are you have not been keeping your packets in a place which is sufficiently cool or dry.
Silverfish	These are dull silver insects the size of a pen nib. They move quickly and are encouraged by crumbs and spillages – an incentive to clean storage areas regularly. Once again they can be killed by fly spray. Although they themselves do not present a particular health risk any infestations should be dealt with promptly.

This is what happens when a fly lands on your food.

Flies can't eat solid food, so to soften it up they vomit on it.

Then they stamp the vomit in until it's a liquid, usually stamping in a few germs for good measure.

Then when it's good and runny they suck it all back again, probably dropping some excrement at the same time.

And then, when they've finished eating, it's your turn.

Cover food. Cover eating and drinking utensils. Cover dustbins.

HEALTH EDUCATION COUNCIL

fast-moving insects, a very good way of catching them without crushing them is to dab them on to a slightly damp bar of soap.

Finally there are house flies which are the commonest insect pests and probably the dirtiest. It goes without saying that these should always be kept out of your cupboards and your kitchen generally.

This Health Education Council poster says it all.

5 COOKING, SERVING AND REHEATING

Why do we cook food? It may seem a silly question but the cooking process is more complex than many of us realise. It alters raw foods and ingredients to make them edible. But it also has another purpose – it makes them safe. For example, when we cook meat we not only make the fibres of the meat tender, we also allow a whole host of physical, chemical and microbiological changes to take place.

In this chapter we will concentrate on the chemical and microbiological changes that are concerned with food safety. For instance, you may recall from Chapter 3 that boiling red kidney beans for 10 or more minutes destroys the chemical toxin that would otherwise lead to illness. In the same way, thorough cooking destroys most bacteria, viruses and parasites.

The way we prepare and cook our food is, in a sense, our last line of defence. We have taken care to select good-quality ingredients from hygienic shops, they've been transported and stored correctly and used while still fresh but, despite all that, poor hygiene during the preparation and cooking process or in your kitchen can still give bacteria a 'window of opportunity'. Many of the mistakes that ultimately result in food poisoning or illness can occur during the preparation and cooking of food.

PERSONAL HYGIENE: SOME OF YOUR BITS AIN'T NICE

This sub-heading has been purloined from a Health Education Council leaflet on personal hygiene. And it is very appropriate. Good standards of personal hygiene are fundamental to safe preparation and cooking of food and some of these principles may be less obvious than you think.

The first thing to remember, and we

mentioned this in Chapter 3, is that your own skin is covered with millions of tiny bacteria, many of which are capable of causing food poisoning, given half a chance. The principal places where these bacteria are found are listed below.

The hands

The unpalatable truth is that, in bacterial terms, our hands are generally 'filthy' and only constant hand washing will keep them clean enough to handle food hygienically.

How then do they become contaminated? Firstly, it is an established fact that up to 40 per cent of healthy adults carry Staphylococcus aureus in their noses and 15 per cent on their hands. There is no way of telling whether you are such a person and this particular bacteria can cause food poisoning if allowed to grow in badly handled or stored food.

Secondly, we use our hands to do just about every imaginable dirty job: emptying the rubbish bin, handling raw foods and poultry (remember 60 per cent of chickens are contaminated with Salmonella), washing dirty vegetables, petting the dog and using toilet paper. The bacteria that you normally excrete when you go to the lavatory can pass through *seven* layers of toilet paper.

WHEN TO WASH YOUR HANDS

Always wash your hands *before* preparing food, and *after* the following tasks while preparing food:

- visiting the loo
- emptying the rubbish bin
- blowing your nose
- touching your hair or face.

Also during food preparation wash your hands *after*:

- handling raw meat
- handling raw vegetables.

As you can see, hands are easily contaminated and can in turn contaminate food quite significantly. The rule must be to keep them scrupulously clean and to handle food as little as possible. Short fingernails also help.

The basic rule for hand washing is to use hot water and soap. In the catering world some companies supply disinfectant soaps but this is usually an expensive waste of money and certainly not necessary in the domestic kitchen. The best way of getting rid of bacteria is to use plenty of hot soapy water and physically wash them off. Then dry your hands on a clean towel although, if you want to be really strict about hygiene, paper towels are much better. A towel, once used, soon ends up as a haven for bacteria, and puts more on our hands than it takes off.

The face

Sad to say, our noses, mouths and hair are all pretty dirty. They harbour food poisoning bacteria in quite high numbers. In fact it could almost put you off the opposite sex (but then, perhaps not). While we're on the subject of the opposite sex, you may be wondering why kissing and other bodily contact doesn't usually cause food poisoning. It is because the bacteria that may be transferred have not had the opportunity to grow to sufficient numbers to cause infection. They have to compete for survival with other bacteria on your skin and are generally not nearly as happy as they are in food. However some strains of Salmonella are sufficiently virulent to cause illness through physical contact. It is not unknown, for example, for mothers to catch Salmonella infection from their children, or vice versa, during nappy changing or feeding.

Spots, pimples and cuts

Spots and pimples are absolutely teeming with food poisoning bacteria, usually our old favourite Staphylococcus aureus. In fact the yellow pus of a spot is such a huge accumulation of normally invisible bacteria that they can now be seen with the naked eye. Ugh! Cuts, spots and pimples, particularly on the hands, should always be covered with a waterproof dressing

until completely healed. Even what most people call a 'clean'
cut should be covered.

Illness

In a commercial kitchen food handlers are legally required to
notify their employer if they've had diarrhoea, vomiting and
one or two other infectious conditions that could be passed on
via food to other people. This principle is just as valid in a
domestic kitchen. If you have got diarrhoea and vomiting, try
to avoid preparing food for yourself or others. You probably
won't feel like it anyway. If there is absolutely no alternative,
take extra care with personal hygiene, particularly hand washing after visiting the loo. (See Chapter 9 for some sound advice
on what to do if you have 'a dose of the trots'.) On the subject
of personal hygiene, it's also worth considering a few other bad
habits that some of us have.

BAD HABITS

Wiping hands on aprons or clothing

This is a common habit and we all tend to
do it. However if you wipe your hands on
your sleeves or apron (particularly after
you've been handling such things as raw
meats) it's quite likely that you'll have left
Salmonella or other bacteria all over the
apron. Washing your hands afterwards
cleans your hands, but as soon as you
touch your apron again, they are recontaminated. If your
hands are dirty wash them, don't wipe them.

Tasting with fingers

It's natural to taste food while you're preparing it – to check
the spiciness of the sauce or soup or stock, or whatever.
But you should never dip your fingers into the food or dip
a spoon or utensil that you've just put into your mouth back
into the food. If you do, you could be transferring thousands

of Staphylococci into an otherwise safe well-cooked dish.
During a long cooling period they would multiply
enormously.

Biting fingernails

This is a very difficult habit to overcome and obviously
unhygienic because you are putting your fingers in your mouth
again. You may be interested to know that some catering
companies refuse to employ staff who bite their fingernails.
If you have this problem there is little advice we can offer,
other than to tell you it is a most unhygienic habit if you are
handling food regularly.

Touching the face

As we know, the face harbours potentially harmful bacteria in
large numbers. For this reason you should always avoid touching your face while preparing food, taking special care not to
scratch or touch your nose, hair or mouth.

Smoking

Smoking also entails putting your fingers to your mouth and
should therefore be banned from the kitchen. Leaving aside the
personal health risks associated with smoking, how would you
feel if you were standing at a servery in a restaurant or
motorway service station and the food handlers spat on their
fingers before serving you? In bacterial terms, that's just what
you do when you smoke.

Wearing jewellery

Jewellery shouldn't be worn when handling food. You may
have noticed that the skin underneath a ring often gets soft-
ened and slightly tacky – this is an accumulation of bacteria.

CROSS-CONTAMINATION

Some bacteria have the ability to move around but only micro-
scopic distances. They cannot move around a kitchen without
help from us. 'Cross-contamination' is a technical term used by

Environmental Health Officers and Food Hygienists to describe how bacteria are moved from place to place. Usually this is from somewhere that we know bacteria are likely to be found (e.g. raw meats) to somewhere where they clearly shouldn't be (e.g. cooked meats).

For cross-contamination to occur, you need a source of bacteria. We have covered all the main areas but, to recap, the sources generally found in a domestic kitchen are:

- raw foods – especially meat and poultry but also unwashed vegetables
- pets and animals
- people, especially their hands, faces and noses
- bins, rubbish and dirty areas
- pests, especially rodents and flies
- laundry.

For illness to result you then have to transfer the bacteria from one of these sources to food that will be eaten – particularly if it is going to be eaten without further cooking. The transfer can take place in one of two ways: direct or indirect. Direct contamination is straightforward – for example putting raw meat above cooked food in a refrigerator and allowing blood to drip down and contaminate foods below. Remember, it may not always be obvious that this has happened. And if you doubt its importance, consider the case of a chef in a restaurant in Bristol who made the mistake of storing raw chicken livers above a large bowl of pâté. The meat juices from the chicken livers dripped down through the fridge and into the bowl of pâté. The juices were contaminated with Salmonella (as over 60 per cent of raw chickens are), and had therefore found their way into an ideal environment for growth. The chef compounded his first mistake by leaving the bowl of pâté out of the fridge during lunchtime and evening trading sessions. As the pâté warmed up, the Salmonella had a field day, multiplying in their millions and subsequently making well over 100 people ill. The chef was sacked and the restaurant closed.

Indirect cross-contamination is much more difficult to spot and control. The main danger areas in your kitchen are listed below.

Hands

We have already established that your hands are commonly contaminated with bacteria that have the potential to cause food poisoning. This is either from 'natural' contamination found on the skin or as a result of handling raw meats and other dirty items.

Knives and utensils

It is always important to wash knives and utensils after use but you must be particularly careful not to use the same knives and equipment to prepare both raw and cooked food. In catering establishments hygiene-conscious chefs use colour-coded equipment to be absolutely sure they never make this mistake. At home, most people have their favourite knives for various jobs anyway, and it's easier to control than a commercial kitchen full of busy staff.

Chopping boards

These can be a menace unless you are particularly careful. Under a microscope the surface of your chopping board will resemble a mountainous region full of nooks, crannies and caves that hundreds and thousands of bacteria can hide in. As with the knives and utensils, it's best to have chopping boards that are used for separate activities and are easily distinguishable from one another. If only one board is available then at least use different sides for cooked and raw foods. Plastic chopping boards (which can be put in the dishwasher) are now available, and are much easier to keep clean.

Cloths and sponges

If you really want to spread bacteria all over your kitchen, use a dish cloth! Unless wiping cloths and sponges are regularly disinfected they can spread more bacteria than they remove. If you think about it, it's obvious. You wipe down a work surface or chopping board that has had raw chicken on it. The sponge or cloth picks up Salmonella which suddenly finds itself in an ideal environment. The sponge is like a holiday home for Salmonella. It's moist, warm, has plenty of nooks and crannies to hide in, and there will be an ample supply of food because you have been cleaning and wiping up bits and pieces with it. Anything you subsequently wipe down with that particular cloth will have Salmonella spread all over it and if you leave the cloth in the warm kitchen for a few hours they'll be multiplying in their millions.

Disposable paper is a much better option for wiping and mopping up. If you must use something else, then wash it thoroughly in hot water or a solution of bleach. We deal with cleaning in more detail later in this chapter.

Tea towels

Tea towels are another classic source of contamination. In commercial premises they are strongly discouraged and most professional caterers again use paper towels for final polishing and drying of glasses. The safest method of washing up relies on evaporation or air-drying of crockery. In other words, simply leave the dishes to dry in the dishwasher or on a draining rack. This practice should be particularly popular with your kids who now have a perfect excuse not to do the 'drying-up'.

Washing machines and tumble dryers

Something you should never see in a commercial kitchen is a washing machine. But of course they are very commonly found in domestic kitchens and in many cases there is nowhere else to put them. The problem is quite obvious if you think about it. You'll be bringing contaminated clothing (underwear and so on) into a place that should be scrupulously clean and it's very easy to put the washing down on a work surface, forgetting that you might be leaving bacteria there.

If you can, move the washing machine, tumble dryer and laundry basket out of the kitchen to a utility room. If this is impossible do your washing at a time other than when you are preparing food. Remember not to put dirty clothing on work surfaces and wash your hands after loading the washing machine. (For further details on hygienic kitchen design you can turn to Chapter 7.)

Hygiene rules in the kitchen

You can minimise cross-contamination by observing the following rules:

- Never use the same equipment or surfaces for preparing raw and cooked food, especially meat and poultry.
- Keep raw and cooked food completely separate. Raw foods, such as poultry, are often contaminated with harmful bacteria.
- If you must store raw and cooked food together, keep the cooked above the raw. That way, the blood or possibly contaminated fluids cannot drip into the cooked food and recontaminate it. Cover food wherever possible as this helps prevent accidental contamination.
- Keep insects, rodents, pets and birds out of the kitchen, particularly when you are preparing food. They have very unhygienic habits and can spread bacteria from place to place.
- Maintain the highest standards of personal hygiene.
- Maintain the highest standards of cleanliness.

Kitchen hygiene

Cleanliness, it is said by the more severe among us, is next to godliness. But like personal hygiene, cleaning is fundamental to good standards of food safety. Most domestic kitchens fare well in this respect, particularly when compared with their commercial equivalents. In a recent *Which?* survey (March 1989), 14 domestic kitchens were rated 'good' or 'very good' as opposed to six restaurant kitchens.

However keeping kitchens bacteriologically clean, rather than visually clean, is quite difficult. Remember we can't see bacteria and we've already learnt how easy it is to spread them from place to place with wiping cloths and the like. So here are a few tips that will help you do a more efficient job.

Effective cleaning

There are *three* clear stages to go through if you're going to clean anything effectively.

Step 1: Washing Hot water and a detergent are all that is required here and most of the well-known brands are capable of doing the job properly. A detergent is a chemical substance which actually helps break up grease and improves the ability of water to wash it off. Common examples of detergents found in the home are washing-up liquids and soap powders. (Traditional soap is not really a detergent but it acts in a very similar manner.) One important thing to realise about detergents is that they only remove dirt; they have no effect whatsoever in killing bacteria, they simply wash them off.

To wash things properly, you need to use a clean cloth and a clean bowl or bucket to mix your detergent. Otherwise, any germs or bugs on your cloth or bucket will just be mixed around in the water, and you'll spread them all over your work surfaces. Use very hot water. Hot water kills bacteria and a simple guide is to have the water so hot that you need to use rubber gloves.

Once the water has become dirty or started to cool off, change it. Unless you do so, the bugs will start to survive in the water and you'll be spreading them round again.

Step 2: Disinfection Disinfection is the process by which we kill bacteria and in the home kitchen this is done using either very hot water or chemicals. It's worth noting that disinfection is quite different from sterilisation. Disinfection actually means reducing the numbers of any bacteria to a level where they cannot do us any harm. Sterilisation means killing *all* bacteria. In domestic kitchens we can usually only achieve disinfection.

Despite the claims that some household disinfectants kill all known germs dead, this isn't always practical.

We've already removed the food supply by washing away the dirt and grease and probably killed quite a few bacteria with the hot water. But disinfection is the next stage of the process, where we get a really good job done. It's still important to use very hot water and you will obviously need rubber gloves.

Probably the most effective disinfectant that you can use in a home kitchen is common bleach. The proper name for bleach is hypochlorite, and it works by releasing chlorine, which is a very effective bacteria killer. Chlorine and chlorine-like compounds are of course used for disinfecting swimming pool water. Small quantities of chlorine are added to our drinking water for the same purpose. Chlorine is also very fast-acting and in the proper concentrations it will disinfect a work surface in a couple of minutes.

Bleach has quite a strong smell to it and if you use it neat it could taint food. However, used correctly at the dilution recommended by the manufacturers (usually given on the side of the bottle) it is effective and will not taint food. Bleach breaks down to form salt, so any residue will not be poisonous. Unfortunately it is also easily broken down by dirt or food and is only really effective on a clean surface. Furthermore, many detergents can affect its performance, and it attacks some metals. It should therefore be used with care and rinsed off afterwards.

On the subject of disinfectants, pine disinfectants are of little value for cleaning work surfaces and key areas, unless you happen to like their smell and don't mind pine taints on your food.

The rules for the use of disinfectants are very similar to those for detergents:

- They work best at high temperatures.
- Never add fresh disinfectant to an old solution.
- Keep using fresh solution (they soon stop working if the water has become dirty).

Step 3: Drying This is the last stage in the cleaning process. Most bacteria don't survive well on a dry surface but thrive on a wet one. If you are using really hot water for washing and disinfecting, the surface or equipment should evaporate dry with little extra help. If you do need to assist with drying then a wipe with a disposable paper towel is probably best.

What to clean and when

So now we know *how* to clean a kitchen, the next question is *what* to clean, and when. Do you need to disinfect your work surface daily? Is daily disinfection enough? What about chopping boards, floors, knives, drawers, cupboards and fridges? Here are our recommendations based on good science and a lot of common sense.

Work surfaces and chopping boards The rule with your work surfaces is to clean as you go. But it's worth taking extra trouble to disinfect the surface or chopping board after you've prepared raw meats or any raw foods, and *before* you prepare any cooked food. Remember that it's almost impossible to clean a wooden cutting board effectively. The surface becomes scored very quickly and bacteria hide in the cracks and crevices.

Fridges and freezers These should be regularly cleaned and defrosted, and if any blood from raw meat has leaked out on to the surfaces they should be disinfected with bleach. However you need to be careful not to use too strong a solution or you will taint food (especially fats) with the smell of bleach. Generally speaking, fridges are better cleaned with bicarbonate of soda as this does not cause taint problems.

Once you've cleaned and disinfected your fridge or freezer it must be dried. Otherwise the few bacteria that are left will multiply again. Bacteria grow very rapidly on anything which is left damp or wet.

Utensils and equipment These should always be cleaned after use but be especially careful about cross-contamination. Knives and equipment used for raw food should be cleaned particularly carefully. (For further details see the section on 'Washing-up' below.)

Sinks As food is sometimes prepared in the sink it's important to keep the internal surfaces clean. The three-step method (wash, disinfect and dry) is adequate for the sink. But if you want to use it immediately you can miss out the drying stage, and rinse it with clean hot water instead.

One piece of advice about plug holes and drains – many manufacturers of bleach or disinfectant advise you to pour it down plug holes and drains. This is little more than a con. Sink wastes and drains are trapped with a U- or S-bend to stop germs and smells getting into the kitchen. It's true that the water in the trap will be teeming with millions of bacteria but they present no risk as they cannot get out of the trap and into the kitchen or on to your food. If you do try to kill them, by pouring bleach or boiling water down the plug hole, they'll be back in their millions within hours. For those who have smelly drains, bleach or disinfectant is not the answer. The drain is probably blocked.

Floor The floor certainly needs to be kept clean, particularly around the edges, corners and behind equipment you don't often move. Even tiny accumulations of food or grease are a major food source for insects and mice who need very little to survive. It's not generally necessary to disinfect your kitchen floor, except in unusual circumstances (when a pet has left something unpleasant for you in the morning, for example).

Toilets Most people realise that toilets are a place where you'll find plenty of germs. After all bacteria make up approximately one-third of the weight of human faeces. So, in bacterial terms, the loo is a very dirty place. And, just like the plug hole, even using gallons of expensive toilet cleaner has a limited effect. As soon as anyone uses it the bacteria are all over the pan again. Just to make you feel even more squeamish, when you flush the loo it produces a fine mist of water droplets which carry bacteria all round the bathroom. This is one reason why toilets have to have a ventilated lobby between them and any kitchen.

But let's not get neurotic. The main problem, in terms of food hygiene, is cross-contamination via your hands. Bacteria are likely to be found not only in the toilet pan, but also on the door handle, flushing levers and basin taps. So while it's worth disinfecting these on occasion (especially when there is a tummy bug running round the family) the best protection is to wash your hands thoroughly not only after visiting the loo but again before you prepare food.

One other point: in the case of older houses you may be able to get an improvement grant if your toilet or bathroom connects directly with the kitchen. Your local Environmental Health Department or Council will have the details.

Washing-up Washing-up is a straightforward daily chore that most of us do without thinking (although seldom without complaining). The risk of contaminating food from dirty plates and utensils is relatively low in most people's kitchens. But as we do have to do the washing-up we ought to do it properly. Here's the ideal method using a double sink:

- Scrape food residues off into the bin.
- Wash the items in detergent and water hot enough that you feel the need to wear rubber gloves.
- Use a plastic-handled nylon brush. (It's less likely to pick up particles of food than a cloth, which so often becomes a breeding ground for bacteria.)
- Rinse the items in the second sink, containing even hotter water.
- Leave them in the hot sink for a couple of minutes. (This helps kill bacteria and warms the item in preparation for air drying.)
- Remove the items from the rinse sink and leave to air dry. (This avoids recontamination from tea towels and also saves time.)
- Use paper towels to give glasses and cutlery a final polish if you wish.

Later, in Chapter 7, you'll see how Annette Anderson hopes to reorganise her kitchen to improve hygiene standards. One of the changes she plans is to put in a double sink. Not everyone has either the space or the money to make such changes. If that is the case, it's best to scrape and wash the articles as described, but then rinse them under a running hot tap instead of using a second sink. It's not quite as effective and you are likely to use a lot more hot water. But the alternative is to go back to that dirty old tea towel.

Dishwashers Domestic dishwashing machines use chemicals and hot water to clean kitchen articles and, for those that can afford them, they are undoubtedly a labour-saving device. However the manual washing described above, when done properly, is just as effective.

Cleaning chemicals On the subject of cleaning and cleaning chemicals, there are two important rules to remember:

■ Store chemicals safely. (Bleach and most cleaning products are poisonous, and extremely harmful if swallowed, particularly by children.) *Always* lock chemicals away or store them in cupboards that are too high for children to reach.
■ *Never* mix cleaning chemicals. When combined, some of them can release exceptionally poisonous fumes similar to mustard gas which was used to such dreadful effect in the First World War. (There have been one or two such accidents when people have mixed these chemicals, particularly in the toilet. The most recent victim was 'Screaming' Lord Sutch.)

TEMPERATURE CONTROL

Temperature control is probably the single most important factor in the prevention of food poisoning. You must make sure that all foods are:
■ cooked thoroughly
■ cooled quickly
■ and then stored at temperatures which do not encourage bacterial growth.

Remember how quickly bacteria can multiply – in some cases they can double their numbers every 12 minutes. So the time between lunch and dinner is easily enough for them to multiply to a level likely to cause food poisoning.

A very useful piece of research has been undertaken by Dr Diane Roberts of the Communicable Disease Surveillance Centre (CDSC) at Colindale. Dr Roberts is part of a team who produce the confidential Communicable Disease Surveillance Report. They are in the forefront of controlling infectious disease in this country. Only a few years ago the Government considered closing down the CDSC and if it hadn't been for the emergence of Aids and their work in that area the labs may well have been closed. But it is the research work and monitoring of disease undertaken by Dr Roberts and her colleagues that allows us to respond to growing problems like Salmonella enteritidis and Listeria.

Dr Roberts examined the factors that contributed to outbreaks of food poisoning and listed the 10 most common causes. They were:

- *Preparing food in advance and storing it at room temperature.* This allows any bacteria present in the food to multiply while it's waiting to be consumed. It would probably have been safe if cooled quickly and kept in a refrigerator.
- *Cooling cooked food too slowly.* Cooling food too slowly allows any bacteria that may have survived the cooking process, or been re-introduced by subsequent handling, to multiply. This is why cooking very large joints of meat can be a problem. They take hours to cool down.
- *Inadequate reheating of food.* Most, although not all, bacteria can be killed by thoroughly reheating food. Inadequate reheating allows them to survive and potentially cause illness.
- *The use of cooked food which has been contaminated with food poisoning bacteria.* Cross-contamination, remember, is a major cause of food poisoning.
- *Undercooking food.* Generally speaking, meat or joints need to reach a temperature of 75°C before you can be certain that all bacteria are killed.
- *Inadequate defrosting of frozen foods, particularly poultry.* What happens here is that heat is wasted melting ice rather than

killing food poisoning bacteria. With one or two exceptions, which we'll talk about later, you should never cook from frozen.

■ *Cross-contamination from raw food to cooked food.* An example would be putting a pre-cooked joint underneath raw meat in a refrigerator. The raw meat would drip on to the pre-cooked food, contaminating it. And if your reheating is inadequate you might not kill the bacteria. If the food is to be eaten cold the bacteria would survive anyway.

■ *Failing to keep hot food at or above 63°C.* In Chapter 3 we mentioned that bacteria could multiply rapidly at any temperature between 5°C and 63°C (often referred to as the 'danger zone'). Keeping food lukewarm in a saucepan or at the side of the kitchen gives the bugs a wonderful opportunity to grow.

■ *Infected food handlers.* Here is the value of good personal hygiene and all the points we covered in Chapter 4.

■ *Re-using leftovers.* The continual heating, cooling and reheating of food takes it through the danger zone more than once. Each time, any surviving bacteria have yet another chance to multiply and cause illness.

As you look down this list you will realise that temperature control – whether cooking properly or defrosting carefully – features heavily in the 10 most common causes of food poisoning. If there is one thing we would love you to remember above all else it must be the importance of temperature control.

COOKING

Any good recipe book combines cooking temperatures with cooking times. One without the other is of little practical use and the same principle applies to the process of killing bacteria with heat. Except at very high temperatures, bacteria don't die as soon as a particular temperature is reached, but the rate of dying gets faster than the rate of multiplication so there is a net loss. However, once a temperature of 75°C has been reached in the centre of food most bacteria will have been killed and the food should be safe.

The higher the temperature the quicker the bacteria are killed and this means that high-temperature short-time methods of cooking are probably the safest. Some examples are:

■ frying
■ boiling
■ pressure cooking
■ and steaming.

Notice how all these methods are 'wet' styles of cooking. Frying is obviously the hottest with the oil being between 200 and 250°C. But even boiling at 100°C cooks things quickly in comparison to the same temperature in a dry atmosphere.

Slower, lower-temperature methods are not as effective at killing bacteria. Some examples are:

■ stewing
■ roasting
■ and baking.

However we can double-check the slower methods of cooking by using an oven or skewer thermometer which guarantees that you have reached the correct centre temperature of 75°C. Most cookery books describe meat cooked to a temperature of 75°C as well done, around 70°C as medium, and 60°C as rare.

Rare meat

Don't worry, we're not advocating cooking everything to death just because Salmonella might be present. Many people like their meat rare (especially beef) and you'll be glad to know that this is still safe. In Chapter 3 we described how meat might be contaminated in the slaughterhouse. Such contamination usually occurs on the *surface* and solid lumps of meat seldom have bacteria in their centre. This means that, although you don't cook the *centre* of a large joint to 75°C, the outside of the meat will have reached a safe temperature and most of the Salmonella or other bacteria will have been killed. Traditional methods of cooking, like Beef Wellington, have usually stood the test of time and you don't need to become so hygiene-conscious that you put yourself or your friends off good food.

To recap, solid pieces of meat such as beef or lamb joints can be cooked rare because there are not likely to be any germs in the centre.

Rolled and stuffed joints These require different treatment from solid joints. You must always thoroughly cook anything that has been boned and rolled, or stuffed. When you roll meat, bacteria on the outside are rolled into the centre, where they're protected from the heat. Also the stuffing is handled quite a lot before it's pushed into the centre of the meat and can therefore easily become contaminated. Most Environmental Health Officers recommend only stuffing the neck of a turkey at Christmas. This allows the hot air to circulate properly on the inside of the carcass as well as the outside.

Pies and minced meat dishes Always thoroughly cook pies or other meat products made with small or minced pieces of meat. Once again, you will have spread the bacteria that are normally on the outside all over the rest of the meat. The mincing process mixes up all the spoilage bacteria in just the same way and mince can therefore go off very quickly.

COOLING

Cooling food quickly is very important. When you first cook something it's most unlikely that you will actually sterilise it. That is to say, you probably won't kill *all* the bacteria that are present. Usually a few will survive, although not enough to make anyone ill. But as the meat cools down from the high temperatures that the bacteria don't like it begins to enter the danger zone. The bacteria find themselves, once again, in the ideal environment and start to multiply.

However they can't do this straight away. It takes them a while to realise all is well and microbiologists call this the 'lag phase' – generally estimated at about 1½ hours. So if you never leave food to cool for longer than 1½ hours the bacteria never really reach their optimum growth phase. Just about the time they decide all's well and it's time to start multiplying you pop the food into the fridge and spoil the whole thing! The fridge brings the food down to 5°C and growth of bacteria slows to a virtual standstill.

As we mentioned earlier, domestic fridges cannot cope well with cooling any sizeable quantity of hot food. If you put too much hot or warm food in a small fridge you warm all the other foods and wake up the otherwise dormant bacteria in them. Here are a few tips for cooling food quickly and safely:

■ Break bulk by cutting the food up into smaller pieces or dividing it into several portions.

■ Place saucepans of hot food in a sink of ice or cold water.

■ Cook smaller quantities or joints below 3 lb, as they will cool more quickly.

REHEATING

It's not usually a good idea to reheat leftovers, especially if you have not cooked the food thoroughly and/or cooled it quickly. We have seen that re-using leftovers is one of the 10 most common causes of food poisoning because cooking, cooling and reheating continually takes food through the danger zone (5°C to 63°C). For this reason reheated food is never as safe as freshly cooked food. In particular, you should avoid eating reheated food that has been:

■ standing around unrefrigerated for more than 1½ hours (certainly not if it has been left to cool overnight)

■ or handled a lot (this may have introduced contamination).

If you must reheat food, make sure you do it thoroughly. This will kill most bacteria including Salmonella, but toxins from bacteria like Staphylococcus or Bacillus cereus will not be destroyed.

THAWING

Thawing food properly is important. Undertaken incorrectly, it can lead to serious undercooking or heavy bacterial growth. There are two basic rules:
■ thaw food thoroughly so no ice remains
■ thaw food under controlled conditions, i.e. in a refrigerator or over a short period of time (usually in a microwave).

Thawing thoroughly is particularly important where large joints of meat and poultry are concerned. A lot of extra heat is required to change ice to water. Therefore if ice remains in the food, heat is wasted on melting it. As we have said, this can lead to serious undercooking and survival of harmful bacteria. If poultry is properly thawed the legs should move freely and no ice crystals should be felt in the meat.

Thawing under controlled conditions prevents excessive growth of bacteria. Food thaws from the outside inwards and so the surface (where most bacteria are likely to be found) warms up into the danger zone. While the inside is still thawing, on the outside the bacteria are multiplying. For this reason you are advised to thaw food in a cool place, preferably in a refrigerator.

Unfortunately, large items can take several hours to thaw in the refrigerator. So try to plan ahead and leave yourself enough time for defrosting. Alternatively, if you have a microwave with a defrost cycle, you could use that. As microwave ovens vary in their power rating we advise you to check the manufacturer's handbook for the correct time and temperature. (And see the section on defrosting in a microwave in Chapter 7, page 117.)

Having read Chapters 4 and 5, you might well be asking how anyone ever survived before paper towels, dishwashers, plastic chopping boards, cold boxes and so on. The answer is simple and repeats a point we made in the Introduction – everyone got on very well when they knew the basic rules of food handling

Defrosting safely

Here are a few useful tips on defrosting food:

- Loosely cover the food (particularly cooked food) with aluminium foil or greaseproof paper during defrosting in order to help prevent cross-contamination.
- Avoid continual freezing, thawing and re-freezing of food. At home the thawing/freezing process is slow and this inevitably means that food stays in the danger zone for long periods.
- Throw away thawed liquids from meat and poultry, and watch out for cross-contamination (for example, thawed liquids dripping on to other foods).
- Don't re-freeze food after a freezer breakdown or power cut. Most home insurance policies offer cheap cover for the contents of a freezer. If you do have a power cut leave the lid closed as this helps keep the cold in.
- Only freezers with a four-star rating are suitable for home-freezing of fresh foods. Freezers with fewer stars can only be used for storage. The star ratings are as follows:
  - *   one week
  - **   one month
  - ***   three months.

and when food was not mass-produced in such a way as to heighten the risk of contamination. But if obeying the rules of food hygiene seems impossibly complicated to you then bear this in mind: we are not saying you need to go in for any *extra* work – we are just advising you to do what you already do . . . but more *safely*. It really is that simple. Remember that we have total control over our own kitchens.

Now how about extending this same good sense to all your family's activities? Read on.

6 FAMILY AFFAIRS

Having talked about buying, storing and cooking food, it has to be said that the average household presents many other potential hygiene hazards. In this chapter we look at the particular problems associated with babies, children and family pets. We also look at the more unusual kinds of catering such as picnics, barbecues and larger parties.

BABIES

In the first few weeks of life babies are especially vulnerable to stomach disorders and food poisoning. The harmless bacteria that inhabit their gastro-intestinal tract, and compete with more harmful organisms, have yet to establish themselves. Furthermore, the baby's infection control system is only just gearing up to cope with life outside the warm and protective environment of its mother's womb.

Breast-feeding

Few hard and fast rules can be laid down about feeding infants and it's not the purpose of this book to discuss the merits of the breast versus the bottle. However, though fashions come and fashions go, there can be no doubt that breast milk provides an excellent food for babies. It's a marketing manager's ideal product! The milk is handily packaged, easily dispensed, portable and always at the right temperature. In addition, breast milk contains antibodies which help the baby fight infection in its first months of life.

Some foods, if eaten by the mother, will affect the baby via her breast milk and can occasionally cause skin problems or diarrhoea. Certain types of fruit (particularly acidic ones like grapes), fizzy drinks, wine and spicy foods like curry have all been documented as foods which can have such effects. But if a mother suspects these are causing problems, simple trial and error should be enough to identify the cause.

Medicines can also pass through breast milk in small amounts and may sometimes have immediate or long-term effects on the baby. For example, if the mother is taking penicillin there is a possibility that the baby may become sensitised to the drug and perhaps develop an allergy to it later in life. If in doubt the best advice is to check with a doctor.

Very few hygiene problems arise with breast-feeding although the mother should take good care of her breasts and clean the nipples after each feed. Many mothers persuade their babies to release the nipple by popping a finger gently into the baby's mouth. For this reason they should also be careful to have clean fingers and short fingernails.

Bottle-feeding

Bottle-feeding does, of course, have its advantages. For example, the mother can judge exactly how much milk the baby is getting and the father can help with feeding. However hygiene is vital at every stage of bottle preparation, as this is obviously a time when the milk may become contaminated. Warm milk is an ideal medium for bacterial growth and you must take the greatest care if potentially serious infection is to be avoided.

Sterilising In Chapter 5 we agreed that disinfection was all that was normally possible in the home. With babies in the house we have to go a stage further and aim for sterilisation, meaning no bacteria at all. As always, personal hygiene is extremely important. Wash your hands thoroughly and dry them on a clean paper towel before making up any feeds. For thorough cleaning and sterilising you can follow these steps:

- Rinse all the equipment under cold water.
- Scrub it with a bottle brush in warm water and washing-up liquid.
- Teats must be thoroughly washed, inside and out. (Putting salt inside and massaging the teat between finger and thumb helps get rid of any hidden milk and fat particles.)

- Rinse all the equipment thoroughly.
- Make up the sterilising solution according to the manufacturer's instructions.
- Use a sterilising container large enough for all the bottles, teats, rings and tops, as well as the jar and spatula for mixing the formula. (For the solution to be effective all equipment must be completely submerged.)
- Leave the equipment in the solution for the length of time recommended by the manufacturer – usually 1 to 3 hours. (Always check their instructions.)
- Rinse off the solution in cold water.
- After sterilisation make sure you only touch the outside of the bottles and the rim of the teats.
- Keep the equipment on a clean surface until you make up the bottle feed again.

Boil-sterilising As an alternative to sterilising solutions, it is possible to boil-sterilise equipment. Put all the equipment into cold water and bring it to the boil. Some of the equipment will float so make sure it is weighed down under a cup. You will need to boil everything for at least 10 minutes. After this time remove the equipment (using kitchen tongs) and don't leave anything in the water to cool down gradually. Put everything on to a clean surface until you make up the feed.

Making up the formula Having sterilised your equipment and washed your hands you are now ready to make up the feed. Once again you can follow a simple series of steps:

- Use freshly boiled water to make up the feed.
- Mix the powder and water in a cleaned and sterilised bottle or jug. (Follow the instructions for quantities.)
- Seal the bottle with an upside-down teat and cap.
- Cool the milk down quickly by immersing the bottle in clean cold water.
- When cool to the touch, put the bottle in the fridge.

If you are using liquid formula in a tin, scald the top of the tin with boiling water before opening. Using a sterilised tin opener, pierce two holes in the lid (one to let the air in and the other to let the formula out). Then make up the bottle according to the manufacturer's instructions.

Once again, cool the mixture down and refrigerate as soon as possible. If no fridge is available bottles must be made up as required and used quickly.

Cow's milk Cow's milk is not suitable for very young babies but from six months onwards diluted cow's milk can be used. Even then you must still follow the sterilising routine described above.

Using a dummy

Most babies suck their thumbs, fingers or a dummy. Whatever the case, make sure their thumbs and fingers, and particularly the dummy, are clean. Dummies can easily get contaminated and are often found on the living room floor or down the side of a cushion. So they should be sterilised regularly.

Solid baby foods

Most babies begin to take a little solid food when they are between three and six months old. You will probably try various foods (bought or home-made) but you should not keep open jars of food for more than 24 hours, even in the fridge.

There is no such problem with dried baby food. Small quantities of dry food can be made up as needed and then discarded if not eaten.

■ *Home-made baby foods* With the advent of blenders, mixers and food processors, many mothers are now able to prepare their own puréed baby foods. This is fine but we suggest a few more precautions than you will find in most cook books. (For example, one book from a major supermarket simply suggests rinsing the blender goblet in hot water before preparing baby food.) First make sure that the blades and all other parts of the machine have been thoroughly cleaned in the normal way. Then we recommend that freshly boiled water is left to stand in the blender for five minutes (you will have to check that your blender is able to tolerate this temperature).

Again, most cook books give little hygiene advice regarding unused home-made baby food, except that it can be frozen in one-meal portions. This is acceptable but the food must be cooled quickly (certainly within 1½ hours) into very clean containers. And remember to defrost and reheat it thoroughly.

Finally, some recipes include chicken, meat and raw eggs. The recent problems with Salmonella enteritidis make caution advisable here. You should always ensure that any chicken is well cooked. If a recipe contains raw or lightly cooked eggs then it is best avoided until the Government issues further guidance and can assure us that vulnerable groups, like the very young, can eat raw or lightly cooked eggs safely.

CHILDREN

Children may not be quite as vulnerable to infection as babies but there are still plenty of hygiene hazards to look out for.

Nappies and potties

Nappies and potty training all involve potential contact with faecal material. At the risk of repeating ourselves, it's very important to remember personal hygiene when changing nappies. Here are a couple of bad examples to illustrate the point:

- allowing babies to eat while sitting on a potty (small children sometimes like to play with faeces or urine and there is obviously a risk of contamination from fingers to food)
- holding safety pins in your mouth while changing a nappy (this means putting your fingers to your lips when they are highly likely to be contaminated from the child's faeces).

These are not major issues but show how a little extra care and thought could help avoid illness, either for the child or the parent.

Playing in the house and garden

All children put things in their mouths – it's part of the process of growing up and developing sensory skills. The inside of the mouth is very sensitive and that's partly why children find the mouth so useful to experience objects and to learn about tastes and shapes. It is common sense not to let children put anything dirty in their mouths. And you should be particularly careful if there is a pet about the house, especially a dog. (See the section on 'Pets' later in this chapter, page 110.)

COOKING FOR LARGE NUMBERS

From time to time most home cooks will end up with the unenviable task of preparing food for a family wedding, birthday party, anniversary or just tea for a cricket or football match. Organising food for large numbers always requires extra care. Functions are notorious for causing some pretty large outbreaks of food poisoning. Even professional caterers have been known to make some awful gaffes.

The Problems

Once again, the problems really boil down to temperature control and cross-contamination, *particularly temperature control.* If you are catering for large numbers all sorts of new problems present themselves.

Preparation The need to prepare large quantities creates two major problems. Firstly, you'll probably be calling for help from friends and family, and two or more people working together in a domestic kitchen can increase the possibility of accidental cross-contamination.

Secondly, there is a temptation to cook the largest possible quantities to save time. Very large saucepans or pots of food can prevent air reaching the bottom of the saucepan, creating conditions that some bacteria find particularly suitable. Also, large joints of meat or poultry can take a long time to cook and, as you will be working with unfamiliar quantities, there is a greater risk of accidental undercooking.

Cooling Temperature control is crucial. Remember the danger zone from Chapter 5? We have already suggested breaking bulk to help cool food quickly and this is even more important when catering for large numbers. But you may not have enough refrigeration space and containers to do this effectively. The fridge will almost certainly be overloaded, reducing its efficiency. There may not even be room in a small domestic fridge for some large items like a 25 lb turkey.

Serving Every chef understands that people 'eat with their eyes' so good presentation is undoubtedly very important, but what about temperature control? Once again, dealing with large numbers increases the temptation to serve up food early. And this means an absence of any temperature control while it sits around on tables for hours on end.

So here we have more problems than normal to deal with – but don't despair. There are some practical hints that we can offer. If in the end you chicken out and call in outside professional help, make sure that they know how to handle food. Environmental Health Officers often have people turn up at the Town Hall with airy-fairy ideas about setting up catering businesses. Almost inevitably they see themselves catering for weddings and the like. A glance through a local paper will identify any number of small function caterers and you should always ask them how they intend to deal with the problems outlined. A few pointed questions will suffice and if the answers are vague or woolly our advice is to go elsewhere.

The Solutions

If you don't have the right facilities there is no magic wand we can wave to help you prepare food safely. However, the following advice should be useful.

Preparation Many hands make light work and it may be worth farming out some of the tasks to friends and family. To reduce the risks of cross-contamination, try to prepare cooked and raw foods at completely different times.

You may decide to choose low-risk items for your menu. For example, avoid large poultry such as turkey, and big joints of meat. Stick to small items that can be cooked well in advance and can also be chilled or frozen, defrosted and reheated easily. Stir large saucepans vigorously to ensure uniform heating.

Prepare rice and savoury salads as late as possible. Cool rice down quickly by rinsing it in cold water and refrigerating.

Storage Ask neighbours and friends for help with cold storage in refrigerators and freezers, but avoid moving lots of food around if you can't keep it well chilled or frozen during the journey. Always cool food quickly.

Empty your fridge of all non-essentials. For example, you can store wine and beer in a cold box. If there's a lot of wine put it in the bath with several bags of ice. Food can also be kept in cold boxes at a pinch (and it's worth putting the ice packs at the top of the box because cold air sinks).

Serving Put the food out on plates as late as possible. Try to have it on display for only a few hours and then clear it away. You will certainly be taking a risk by leaving high-risk foods on an unrefrigerated buffet display all day, especially in summer months. (See Chapter 9 page 160 for a case in point.) Remember, food poisoning statistics always rise during the summer. If you really have to put food out early, then put out the low-risk items like crisps, peanuts, bread and cakes (not ones containing fresh cream).

Hot food can be a problem if you don't have special equipment. There are no easy answers here but heated trays can help. Use metal trays as these help to transfer heat from the tray to the food.

Leftovers Leftovers should be thrown away. The food has been unrefrigerated for many hours and mauled by many hands. Don't be tempted to keep it.

To recap, think hygiene, think temperature control, and you

should be all right. If you have a really big function, especially for a local gathering, it may be worth asking your Environmental Health Officer for some advice on hygiene. They are usually pretty busy but prevention is always better than cure. A little helpful advice could save a lot of effort later on when they are called to investigate your outbreak of food poisoning.

The law

You should remember that food prepared for fêtes, local functions, etc. definitely comes under the umbrella of food hygiene legislation. This is another reason for involving the Environmental Health Officer in a major event. Prosecution or legal action is unlikely but not impossible if serious mistakes are made. (For a summary of the relevant law you can turn to Chapter 9, page 166.)

BARBECUES

When summer arrives many of us begin rummaging in the garage or garden shed to dust off the barbecue. If popular folk law is to be believed, the 'barbie' has been an integral part of Australian, American and Canadian life for many years and it has undoubtedly become more popular in Britain as well. At first glance you would think barbecued food would be particularly safe as it involves a high-temperature, short-time method of cooking. The hot coals produce an incredibly fierce heat that can certainly deal with even the hardiest bacteria or toxin.

But, of course, life is not as simple as that. With any form of cooking, we can make mistakes. For example, the heat of a barbecue is sometimes so fierce that the inexperienced chef can cremate the outside of the food while leaving the inside undercooked. As we mentioned earlier, this is probably acceptable for solid pieces of meat. But one of the popular items for barbecuing will be home-made beef burgers which essentially consist of minced meat. Potentially harmful bacteria will still be in their centre. Once again, good hygiene means knowing where bacteria might be and taking a little more care as a result.

Risky items

Some foods are clearly riskier than others to cook on the barbecue. Manufactured beef burgers can be safely cooked from frozen because they are relatively thin and the heat can penetrate the meat easily. Conversely, home-made burgers are generally much thicker and should be really well cooked.

Poultry can be cooked safely on a barbecue, although extra care is needed because of the high level of Salmonella contamination found in it. Make sure that chicken is well cooked and kept to one side of other foods before and during the cooking process. We suggest you never use a barbecue for cooking very large pieces of poultry and certainly frozen poultry should never be cooked on the barbecue. It's just too risky, as much of the heat will be wasted melting ice rather than cooking the meat and killing the Salmonella. If you are worried about thorough cooking one tip is to pre-cook large items on the day and then just brown the skin on the barbecue so that it picks up the delicious flavours and aromas without leaving you to worry about whether it is thoroughly cooked.

Apart from ensuring that food is properly cooked on a barbecue, another thing to look out for is potential cross-contamination. When lots of items are being cooked at once, raw and cooked foods can easily get jumbled together on the grill. Fortunately, because the food is eaten so quickly, there is little time for harmful growth to occur on contaminated cooked food. Most healthy adults can cope with relatively small doses of Salmonella and other harmful bacteria but it's still worth avoiding cross-contamination if you can. Although it's uncommon there have been documented cases where very small numbers of Salmonella have caused illness. There's no published data to tell us whether barbecues are a major source of food poisoning or not, but a case we report in Chapter 8 (page 142) shows how carelessness can lead to food poisoning.

Marinades and sauces

It's fine to marinate uncooked items but be careful with the marinade during cooking. It will have been contaminated by the raw foods and if you then brush more marinade on during the cooking process you will recontaminate the food. This is no problem, provided it is well cooked before you eat it.

Sauces should, of course, be refrigerated if they have been prepared in advance. Remember, even thorough cooking on the barbecue will not destroy toxins in sauces contaminated by bacteria like Staphylococcus aureus.

PACKED LUNCHES

Most people think of sandwiches as a perfectly innocuous and very safe food but of course the meat and high-protein fillings are ideal for bacterial growth. That's why reputable super-markets and traders always keep them refrigerated.

Home-made sandwiches should not present any particular problems as long as you have prepared them hygienically (following the rules in Chapters 4 and 5) and eat them within a few hours. If sandwiches are prepared in the morning and eaten at lunchtime (which is the norm) all should be well. But if you are going to take a longer time before eating them then you really have two choices. You can keep the sandwiches cool in an insulated bag or cold box with ice packs. Or you can use low-risk fillings like tinned or bottled sandwich spreads and other foods that are less vulnerable to the growth of bacteria.

PETS

Dogs, cats and other pets are a much-loved part of any family. However animals are natural carriers of a number of diseases that can affect people. There are, therefore, some simple pre-cautions we should take to ensure both their own and our continued health and well-being.

Campylobacter

You may recall from Chapter 2 that Campylobacter is responsible for a greater proportion of stomach upsets than Salmonella. In fact Campylobacter is not really the same as other food poisoning organisms because food is merely one of the routes by which it is picked up. One of the other common routes of infection, and this is where pets come into the picture, is through direct contact. This is especially the case with puppies and kittens that have diarrhoea. Many animals carry Campylobacter, including pigs, cattle, sheep, cats, dogs, rodents, birds and most other pets.

Campylobacter infections among domestic animals and pets can be prevented by proper care and attention, and involvement of the family vet if necessary. Puppies and kittens with diarrhoea are highly likely to be sources of infection, so good personal hygiene after contact with animals is very important. We give some suggestions in the information box below.

On the subject of the organisms domestic pets can carry, even the dear old terrapin and tortoise can be carriers of Salmonella. It's hard to believe that a tortoise can carry Salmonella but it's true and emphasises that good hygiene is essential with any pet.

PET HYGIENE

- Don't let dogs, cats or any pets lick plates or utensils that people eat from.
- Make sure pets have separate feeding bowls.
- As far as possible, keep pets out of the kitchen and certainly don't let cats walk over work tops and work surfaces.
- Clean up pets' faeces and urine immediately and disinfect the area using bleach.
- Maintain good standards of pet hygiene by cleaning out bedding, boxes, cages, etc. on a regular basis.
- Don't allow pets to lick your face and particularly the faces and fingers of children.

Toxicara canis

The potential infection problems associated with dogs and toxicara canis are now much better understood. This is a chronic disease which mainly affects young children. The larvae migrate into the organs and tissues of the body. Infection is very rarely fatal but the most worrying problem is that larvae can enter the eyes and, in some cases, cause partial loss of vision or even complete blindness.

The larvae are transmitted directly or indirectly at the egg stage, often in soil contaminated by the faeces of infected dogs and cats. It's all too easy for children to get such soil on to their fingers and then into their mouths. Surveys have shown that up to a quarter of soil samples from certain parks in the UK contain the eggs. They can survive in the soil for many months. After ingestion they hatch in the intestine and then the larvae penetrate the wall of the intestine, migrating to the liver, the lungs, and from there to other organs. Children are more likely to be infected because they tend to crawl around on the floor and pick up the eggs on their fingers, which they are constantly putting in their mouths.

Almost all puppies will be infected at some time or another by the toxicara canis worm and parents can exercise control in three ways. Firstly, they can de-worm their dogs and cats, beginning at three weeks of age and repeating the process at regular intervals, subject to advice from a vet. Secondly, they can prevent their pets from defecating in areas where children play. Finally, they can make sure their children's hands are clean before eating.

There's obviously a lot we can all do to improve standards of hygiene in our homes. And good kitchen design can make this a great deal easier. In the next chapter we look at one person's attempts to improve her kitchen.

7 TOWARDS THE PERFECT KITCHEN

'Eating out could seriously damage your health but cooking at home may not be as safe as you'd think. A *Which?* report (2.3.89) finds danger lurking in the domestic fridge as well as among restaurant prawn cocktails and Black Forest gateaux. Spot checks on kitchens at 20 central London eating places revealed over 100 hygiene problems . . . but similar checks on 21 home kitchens highlighted ignorance of basic food hygiene and horrors like pet and human food served with the same utensils.'

So ran a press release from the Consumer's Association in March 1989. Those of you who have already read Chapters 4 and 5 will understand the dangers posed by domestic kitchens. Among *Which?*'s more detailed findings were:

- Raw meat above cooked food in the fridge.
- No separate utensils for serving pet food, and pet food stored open in the fridge.
- Fridge temperature 10°C too high (one householder said she had left the door open after taking a yoghurt out).
- Fridge door seal perished.
- Dog and cat running all over kitchen – cat smears and hairs on work surfaces.
- Open-topped plastic bucket used for general rubbish, and cat eating scraps out of it.
- Work surface scored from knife use.
- Food cupboard shelves had accumulations of food debris and dirt.
- Dirty crockery and greasy pans in washing-up bowl, left over from breakfast (inspection at 4.20 p.m.).

The most common causes of food poisoning in the home are

clearly the errors we ourselves make in mishandling food –
chiefly by cross-contamination. We have already looked at safe
practice in the kitchen in some detail. But many of the faults
revealed by *Which?* concern design and equipment. This chapter asks a very important question: *How can we design and maintain our kitchen equipment and kitchens to reduce the danger of
food poisoning?*

To answer this question we are going to look at common
problems with three widely used pieces of equipment – microwaves, ovens and fridges – and then learn about the principles
that are applied to commercial kitchens. Finally, we meet
Annette Anderson from South London who has decided to
redesign her own kitchen to the standards of commercial
premises.

KITCHEN EQUIPMENT

Microwave ovens

Most of the high-technology equipment in
our kitchens began as a luxury and ended
up as a necessity. The latest gadgetry to go
through this familiar metamorphosis is the
microwave. British scientists carrying out
experiments on radar in the war amused
themselves cooking sausages by bombard-
ing them with 'microwaves'. They little imagined that the same
principles would now be employed for a piece of standard kitchen equipment. The Government's Office of Population, Cen-
sus and Surveys (bit of a mouthful that, but civil servants get
upset if you don't give them their full title) reveal in their General Household Survey for 1987 that by the end of that year 30
per cent of homes had a microwave. Manufacturers of microwave ovens, who tend to take the most optimistic view of sales,
say that more than half of British households now have them.
But before we get entirely carried away by the white heat of this
technological revolution let us tell you a cautionary tale.

Lindsay Marie Burdekin is six years old and lives with her

parents, Richard and Pamela, in Shrewsbury. When they heard of the dangers of Salmonella in eggs – on the *Food and Drink* programme in November 1988 – they took it seriously. Richard is the managing director of a food processing plant and he is not likely to be panicked by unjustified scares.

He and his wife decided to stop giving Lindsay scrambled eggs because soft-cooked eggs were included in the Government warnings as representing a risk to small children. Lindsay did not take kindly to her change of diet – she loved scrambled eggs and knew her mother liked cooking them. After all, what could be simpler than a minute and a half in the microwave?

One Friday night in January 1989 Lindsay saw someone eating scrambled eggs on television. It was too much for her – she developed a craving that her parents eventually gave in to. 'It was a decision we would live to regret,' says Richard. Pamela whisked up a couple of eggs and put them in the microwave. She trusted that two minutes (an extra 30 seconds) would cook them solid: 'If there was anything dodgy lurking in the eggs then I figured that extra half minute would zap it.' Lindsay enjoyed every spoonful of her scrambled eggs.

It was not until the Sunday evening, two days later, that she began to feel ill. 'I took her to the doctor's on the Monday,' recalls Pamela. 'He said it was just tonsillitis. He gave her penicillin which made poor Lindsay ten times worse. By now she had dreadful diarrhoea.' So bad was it that the doctor returned that evening and took a sample.

Lindsay had a high fever and as the diarrhoea persisted she became badly dehydrated. Pamela sat up with her all night trying to get her to drink. But when she refused to they had to take her into hospital. There she was persuaded to drink every hour – her mother says the threat of a drip concentrated her mind. Lindsay spent four days in hospital, although it took her three weeks to recover properly.

On the day she came out of hospital the results of the test came through. She had been suffering from Salmonellosis. More specifically the bacterium was Salmonella enteritidis phage type 4 – the strain most commonly associated with poultry and eggs. Having considered the food Lindsay had eaten that weekend, the experts thought the scrambled egg was the most likely culprit.

Richard already knew about the risk in eggs. Apart from kicking himself, he draws another conclusion. Traditional cooking methods are well known to us but people lack experience with microwaves because they are such a new thing. Richard believes that when the Government warned the public about cooking eggs thoroughly they should have mentioned that a microwave might not be able to do the job. After all, Pamela took every precaution by cooking the eggs for longer until they were apparently solid. Richard Burdekin is now wary about using the microwave for any 'short-cook' items because they may not be thoroughly cooked through, thus allowing dangerous bacteria to remain in the food.

Richard may be an angry father but in this case he is not over-reacting. He is absolutely right that microwave ovens represent an additional danger to our health when it comes to food safety. And we all need to understand why. A microwave oven is a shielded container in which food is bombarded by a concentration of microwaves. In part the microwaves agitate the water molecules in the food. This causes heat to build up – it is a process similar to steaming and steam is indeed given off. The microwaves bounce off the walls of the oven so that only the food heats up.

Normally the heat in a microwave penetrates the food more efficiently than conducted heat in a conventional oven. So the advantages of a microwave are speed and efficiency as well as a dramatic saving on the washing of pots and pans. It sounds simple enough, doesn't it? But there are pitfalls, needless to say. If we do not cook our food thoroughly then bacteria can survive. That is the danger.

Dr Colin Smithers has designed microwave ovens and has therefore had to investigate them in some detail. He works for the Cambridge-based technology division of the PA Consultancy Group. These are some of the problems with microwave ovens that he has investigated. They don't invalidate their use but they point up how well we need to understand microwave ovens to get the best out of them:

- *Heat penetration is not as good as we think.* The hottest point is often only 1 to 2 centimetres under the surface. So at the centre of the food it is conduction (as in conventional cooking) rather than microwave penetration that heats the food effectively.
- *Different foods behave differently.*

  Thick soup absorbs microwaves very quickly and cooks intensely at the edge while remaining cool at the centre. It has to be stirred.

  Sponge mixes may not cook evenly.

  Mince pies and other foods with a pastry case stay cold on the outside while they cook inside. This is because pastry is much dryer and therefore has few water molecules to be agitated.

  Meat joints cook quickly just under the surface (see first point above) but need time for the heat to be conducted to the centre.

  Chicken joints and other irregular shapes have a greater surface area than regularly shaped foods of similar volume. They therefore get irregular heating – legs, for instance, would tend to receive rather more heat than other parts of the bird.
- *Most microwaves have 'hot spots' and 'cold spots'.* It is difficult to design an oven in which microwaves are evenly distributed. As a result one part of a dish may be burnt while another remains undercooked. Some of the cheaper models have very pronounced hot and cold spots.
- *Defrosting can be difficult.* The microwaves may successfully defrost a food near its surface. It will then become hot and may even begin to burn, while remaining frozen in the centre. Conductivity (see first point above) is obviously low with frozen food. Defrosting therefore has to be done very slowly. Unevenly thawed food contains a further danger: if you let the outside deceive you into thinking defrosting is complete, and you follow normal cooking times, your food may end up seriously undercooked in the centre. Whatever is lurking there will still be very much alive (some bacteria can survive the deep-freeze).
- *Some timers are unreliable.* Of the two types of timer – the mechanical 'clockwork' and the electronic 'touch-pad' – the for-

mer can be inaccurate. It may be difficult to see easily whether you have dialled up exactly 30 seconds, and it is often physically difficult to set it for times as brief as 15 seconds. Tests of clockwork timers carried out by BBC 1's *Watchdog* programme in 1989 revealed that some clockwork timers are generally unreliable anyway, meaning that they do not always give the cooking time you requested. This is particularly true if you do not load up the spring by turning the knob right round before returning it to your chosen cooking time. (A survey by the Consumers' Association in December 1988 found that this problem still exists in more recent models.)

■ *Cheaper microwave ovens are not so effective.* Some ovens have a wattage as low as 400. These can take a long time to heat and cook food thoroughly. In some cases they are so slow that you might as well use a conventional oven. And if they have no turntable then the food will not be so evenly bombarded by microwaves, ending up less evenly cooked.

■ *Microwaves cannot take standard metal containers.* This point has no relevance to food hygiene but it is worth mentioning here just for safety's sake.

There are a number of techniques we can learn to overcome most of these problems and many of them are carefully documented in the instruction booklets that come with microwave ovens. But how many of us read them thoroughly and then devote the necessary time to learning the techniques for ourselves through practical experimentation?

Debbie Brown is Research Manager of the Consumers' Association Technical and Testing Department where they have carried out countless experiments on microwave ovens over the years. You can consult past editions of *Which?* for best buys; here we are concerned with the best way to use an oven. Many of us already own models. The chances are that they are old, low-wattage, lack turntables and have 'clockwork' timers. We do not want to buy another, more modern oven but we do not want to contract food poisoning either. Debbie Brown has some simple cooking rules to recommend:

■ Instructions which specify 'standing time' after the microwave has turned itself off are very important. This time allows the heat to be conducted through the food evenly.

- When recipes tell you to 'turn the food' make sure you do so. This helps distribute the microwaves more evenly.
- Round dishes also help distribute the microwaves more evenly than square dishes. This is particularly important for meat dishes where bacteria are more likely to lurk. (You may wish to have vegetables only lightly cooked anyway.)

All this advice underlines the importance of reading instructions – both in microwave handbooks and on ready-prepared meals. This is especially true because most microwaves do not brown food when they cook it. And browning is one of the pieces of evidence we normally use to help us judge whether or not food is cooked.

If you do not currently own a microwave but are considering buying one then three features are advisable, even though they will increase the cost:

- electronic digital control (usually touch-pad)
- turntable
- and wave stirrers (rotating antennae).

The first two yield the benefits we have already discussed and are obvious when you look at the model. The third feature is not obvious so it is worth asking about – rotating antennae stir the microwaves around to achieve more even distribution and therefore more even cooking. They work best in conjunction with turntables.

Dr Smithers points out that the most 'state-of-the-art' microwave ovens can now detect the progress of the cooking. They do this either by assessing the humidity content of the air that circulates during cooking, or by detecting temperature changes in the food. This is a feature that is worth asking your dealer about. What you cannot yet ask your dealer about are the ovens which will come on to the market before the end of the century. Not only will many of the features we have discussed be standard but they will employ short-wave technology that achieves greater penetration than does the microwave.

Conventional ovens

The rules that apply to microwave ovens apply to conventional ovens too: undercooking is the great danger. As we saw in Chapter 5, food needs to reach a temperature of 75°C throughout to kill off most of the bacteria that may be lurking within. We can all cook with more confidence when using conventional ovens, partly because we understand them better and partly because they are less complex and more reliable. However, it is not all plain sailing.

Until recently Brian Lawson was a product engineer involved with the testing of ovens at the Cranfield Institute of Technology. He points out that all ovens have a so-called 'dwell' period. If you instruct the oven to cook at 200°C then the thermostat, if it is reliable, will turn off at that temperature. But the response times are generally slow. During this 'dwell' period (known by the boffins as 'hysteresis') the temperature will actually go above 200°C before it comes down again. Likewise, when it does fall and hits 200°C again, 'hysteresis' allows the temperature to fall below 200°C for a while. So your food does not cook consistently at the temperature you have requested. Over a long cooking period this evens itself out so there's no real problem. But what if the thermostat does not work very well?

Even some new ovens have poor thermostats (as Brian Lawson can testify). Many old ovens have thermostats whose performance has deteriorated badly over the years. And a malfunctioning thermostat is likely to make the oven cooler than the desired temperature. What you think is 200°C may in reality be as low as 170°C, and you might seriously undercook your food. So a faulty thermostat could result in food poisoning. If you are not sure of your oven thermostat you can test the food with a meat thermometer (available from any kitchen shop).

A final word of warning about your oven – be critical of every aspect of its operation. Keep an eye out for food that does not seem to cook as you expected. In a March 1989 survey, *Which?* found one new oven that malfunctioned on its defrost option. It actually heated the food to 40°C and melted the chocolate on the outside of a Black Forest gateau while leaving the centre frozen. At 40°C, *Which?* points out, 'the temperature is high enough to cause rapid growth of bacteria – a particular hazard for foods which will not be cooked immediately after defrosting.'

For some reason we do not expect our kitchen appliances to malfunction, and seldom notice when they do. Yet they are merely pieces of machinery with the same frailties as, say, our cars. This is particularly true of the refrigerator. Fridges are a whole new can of worms . . . or, at least, they may well be at the temperature we often allow them to function at.

Fridges and freezers

As we saw in Chapter 4 the fridge plays a vital role in the storage of food. Get it wrong and you are inviting bacteria to multiply at an alarming rate. In its 1988 survey of the nation's food habits (*Food Hygiene*) the Ministry of Agriculture polled a representative sample of 2000 people. They discovered that:

- Only 29 per cent of adults claimed that they ever adjusted the temperature dial in their fridges.
- Only 6 per cent had ever measured the exact temperature in their fridges.

From this we can deduce that most of us are ignorant of the temperature of our fridges; and the *vast* majority of us have never done anything constructive to see whether our fridges are working properly. But what do we mean by 'working properly'?

The agreed international standard for the *average* interior temperature of a refrigerator is 5°C. The word 'average' must be stressed because temperatures will vary inside a fridge. This is because (if you can remember your school physics) heat rises. So any warmer air inside will rise to the top, making that the warmest part and the bottom the coldest. Many people instinctively think the top must be colder because it is nearer the ice box. Not so.

To achieve an average temperature of 5°C, this is what the interior temperatures of your fridge ought to be:

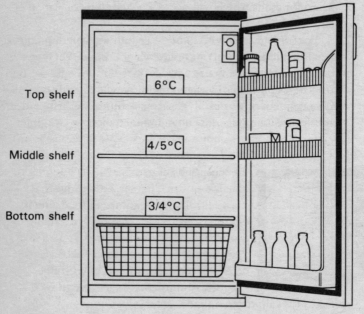

Top shelf — 6°C

Middle shelf — 4/5°C

Bottom shelf — 3/4°C

However if you regularly store such items as cook-chill prepared meals some experts believe that 3°C is the safest average temperature. There are now concerns about the relatively low temperature at which Listeria can multiply (we have already seen that it can survive freezing, as can other bacteria).

In early 1989, at the height of the so-called 'food crisis' when public confidence in the food supply was very low, an enterprising businessman called Colin Rickson carried out a survey of 100 domestic fridges. His company, Liquid Crystal Devices, make and sell thermometers which can be used to check whether fridges are working. So he had every incentive to stoke up public concern about the state of the British fridge. Should we therefore give much credence to his results? The answer is yes, because a local journalist was so surprised by his survey that she checked out the same fridges. Her results were even worse. This is what Rickson found (and remember that the international standard is 5°C):

■ 27 per cent were at 3°C or less (a temperature which would certainly restrain most bacteria from multiplying).

■ 33 per cent were between 7°C and 4°C (around the international standard).

■ 40 per cent were between 8°C and 14°C (at these temperature bacteria would have a field day; and at 14°C the owners may as well not have bothered to use a fridge at all).

It has become quite clear to us while researching this book that the average fridge, despite the much-vaunted British and international standards, is a badly designed piece of equipment which gives us plenty of opportunity to make dangerous errors in our storage of food. Once again, our own inadequacies are only partly to blame. Colin Rickson's survey of 100 households revealed shortcomings all round:

■ Only 15 per cent knew that the correct interior temperature should be 5°C or less.

■ *No one* knew how the numbered temperature dials related to temperature and only 30 per cent were able to guess correctly which way to turn the dial to make the fridge colder (56 per cent actually turned the dial towards defrost to make their fridge colder, in fact making it warmer).

■ 99 per cent did not know the correct temperatures for storing different types of food.

It is very difficult to blame those questioned in the survey for their lack of knowledge when you consider the following four failings. Firstly, there is no standard correlation between temperature dials and temperatures. (Some are 0 to 10, some are 0 to 7, and some are 9 to 1.) Secondly, whatever system is used, there is no chart in the fridge to explain the numbers on the dial in terms of temperature. Thirdly, there is no standard for which way to turn the dial to make the fridge colder, though in most cases the lowest number is the highest temperature. Fourthly, very few fridges have any sort of built-in thermometer device.

In view of all this confusion, what advice can we give you?

If you are in doubt about what your controls mean, turn the dial as far as it will go in the *opposite* direction to the defrost position. It is better to keep food too cold rather than too warm. And you can back off slightly if the milk begins to freeze.

There is also some general advice we can give you to ensure your fridge is functioning properly. These points are particularly important for those who have older models where the thermostat may no longer be reliable:

- *Defrost regularly.* An over-frosted fridge will not operate efficiently.
- *Check that the rubber door seal is not broken.* This can badly compromise the insulation.
- *Don't overload.* If a fridge is stuffed to overflowing it will not be able to cope – the cool air does not circulate effectively and some items will not be chilled properly.
- *Don't leave the door open longer than necessary.* While you are busy in the kitchen it is easy to forget this.
- *Don't put warm dishes in the fridge.* Make sure food is cool first, otherwise the fridge will take *hours* to recover its temperature.
- *Check for dust on the housing at the back.* This can stop the warm air being efficiently removed – the basis principle upon which a fridge works.
- *Position the fridge carefully.* Being placed near the oven or a radiator could seriously affect its performance.

There are far fewer food safety problems associated with fridge-freezers and freezers. Generally speaking, the lower the temperature the longer the food can be stored. (Above 9°C, micro-organisms that can spoil food become active – texture and taste then begin to deteriorate.) The current standard temperature for all freezers is −18°C. Colin Rickson surveyed a number of domestic freezers and found temperatures ranging from −3°C to −26°C.

In its recent surveys of freezers (May 1988) and fridge-freezers (September 1988) *Which?* found a similar problem to the one we have identified with fridges. Few models had built-in thermometers, and even fewer had thermostat controls marked in degrees centigrade. A freezer thermometer is therefore a useful addition to your fridge thermometer. This is particularly important in the light of *Which?*'s discovery that some manufacturers recommended dial settings for their freezers which resulted in temperatures that were too warm.

Zanussi have announced a new model for launch in the summer of 1989 called 'Superchill'. It has a new section for chilled goods which – they claim – keeps food strictly between −1°C and +1°C. Let's hope other manufacturers follow suit.

FRIDGE AND FREEZER THERMOMETERS

To be absolutely sure of interior temperatures buy a fridge or freezer thermometer. There are quite a few models on the market but a *Which?* survey published in May 1989 recommended the Liquid Crystal Display (LCD) thermo-scan fridge thermometer. For freezers, the same survey recommended the Brannon dial freezer thermometer and the Thorpac freezer thermometer (both of which can also be used in the fridge).

Using the thermometers
Place the fridge thermometer on the top shelf of the fridge (the warmest part) for two hours. It should be no more than 5/6°C. With an upright freezer place the thermometer at the top and at the front (its warmest part), and with a chest freezer place it in a basket at the top (its warmest part), again for two hours. It should read −18°C.

KITCHEN DESIGN

Since the Second World War our ideas about kitchens have changed dramatically. Alexander Flinder is the founder of an architectural practice (the Alexander Flinder Ashley Partnership) and he has been a prominent designer of homes for many years. He points out that before the war the average 1930s house had a modest kitchen (effectively a scullery used chiefly as a preparation area). It would be narrow – perhaps no more than 8 feet by 10 feet – with fittings down each side. The dining room (that is, the eating area) was separate.

After the war Flinder designed individual houses for the affluent in such areas as Weybridge in Surrey and Hampstead Garden Suburb in North London. His clients wanted to retain a formal dining room but they also started requesting a less formal eating area where they could breakfast and feed their children. They were influenced, he thinks, by American films and television programmes of the early 1950s showing 'dinettes'. The features which first appear in luxury housing soon become standards for all housing. And what estate agents, with their charming turn of phrase, were to call the 'kitchen-diner' was born. It featured in all the plans of houses constructed in the building booms of the late '50s and '60s.

Kitchens were meanwhile growing bigger for a number of reasons – not just because of a desire to emulate Mr and Mrs Newly-affluent-of-Weybridge. Mothers did not want to be left alone slaving over a hot stove. Husbands coming home from work did not always want to sit on their own in a formal dining room. More and more kitchen gadgetry had to be accommodated – in particular, the fridge. This revolutionary development meant the end of the cool, walk-in larder. And when the pieces of kitchen equipment became so numerous that the room began to resemble a warehouse, the 'fitted kitchen' was born. Local authorities built vast numbers of houses in the '60s and they needed standard kitchen units that were easy to install. This set the seal on the fitted kitchen. In every sense, the kitchen had become a living room.

It would be a mistake to assume that kitchens had never been 'living rooms' before. In fact, throughout civilisation people have been drawn to the kitchen because it has been the best (and often only) source of warmth and food. That cooking Rabbi and *Thought for the Day* star Lionel Blue recalls how Jewish patriarchs would have their coffins made from planks of the kitchen table because this was the most important room in the house.

Until the twentieth century all the working classes in Britain cooked and ate in the same room. As for the upper class and emergent middle class, they may not have done but their servants certainly did. (Do you remember how Hudson and Mrs Bridges practically lived around the kitchen table in *Upstairs Downstairs*?)

In this sense we can regard the age of the scullery (the late nineteenth and the early twentieth century) as the aberration. By making the kitchen a living room once more we have returned to our roots. But there is one vital difference. As we explained in the Introduction our general level of food knowledge, cooking skills and appreciation of food safety are lamentable compared with what they once were. We may be living cheek by jowl with our food and our utensils once more but we have little appreciation of the potential dangers. Today the kitchen sink is likely to have muddy shoes in it, as well as a defrosting chicken. And the dangers are compounded by our ignorance of the new technology that surrounds us. Furthermore, the trend in kitchen design is the open-shelved, 'natural', country-style kitchen (we employ such clichés advisedly). Open shelves and free-hanging pots and pans are not the most hygienic ways of storing utensils.

To underline how low we place food hygiene in our list of priorities we have carried out a modest straw poll. We contacted three suppliers of fitted kitchens in Britain. Two are among the larger suppliers and the third offers a very expensive, individually designed product. We asked them whether they offer any food hygiene advice with regard to layout. These were the replies.

Large supplier 1:
> 'The men installing it might tell you about that.'

Large supplier 2:
> 'No, we have nothing written down.'

Upmarket supplier:
> 'We don't have any advice that I know of. Why don't you ask your local Environmental Health Officer?'

We have checked the brochures of all three companies and we can confirm that food hygiene is not mentioned once. Hygiene considerations may lie behind the designs of their individual units but you would not know it – and you certainly would not get advice on the best layout for food safety.

Faced by what we can only describe as professional incompetence, it is refreshing to meet someone who, entirely on her own initiative, is trying to redesign her own kitchen with food hygiene in mind. Annette Anderson lives with her two teenage children and four cats in South London. Annette trained as a cordon bleu cook at Leith's School of Cookery and then cooked board room lunches for companies. Because she found herself cooking for as many as 70 people at one company she decided to take food hygiene seriously as well. So she attended the relevant courses and now holds a diploma in food hygiene from the Royal Institute of Public Health and Hygiene. Having completed her studies, she turned her mind to conditions nearer her own hearth:

'I'm a pretty bad housewife. I don't like cleaning. I like sitting in the kitchen with a cat on my knee reading a magazine. As likely as not the magazine has an article talking about the classic work triangle – sink, preparation and cooking. But they never seem to mention the hygiene aspect. I've got all this knowledge about food hygiene regulations so why do I have one standard for cooking commercially and another in my own kitchen? Sitting in my kitchen chair I began to wonder whether the food hygiene regulations for commercial kitchens could be used as a basis for designing an ordinary family kitchen. I knew no one would want that cold clinical look that commercial kitchens have in their own home. But there had to be a way of combining the two.'

So Annette decided to have a go. And the first thing she has done is to make an audit of the faults of her current kitchen. As an exercise in self-criticism it would shame even the most ardent follower of Chairman Mao during the Cultural Revolution. But she hopes the process will help her institute a culinary revolution of her own.

At the moment Annette's Victorian terraced house has an old-fashioned scullery opening on to a dining room/seating area which also contains the fridge. Among the faults she has pinpointed are the following (some structural, some organisational and some relating to equipment):

- Bare stripped plaster above the sink where the wall can flake on to the crockery.
- Old exposed pipes harbouring dirt.
- Unhygienic tiling – it ends too low around the sink and food preparation area.
- Old floor tiles – cracked and harbouring dirt.
- No 'production-line' logic, from food storage through food preparation, cooking and serving to clearing up (see below).
- Bare wooden floorboards in dining room retaining dirt and bacteria.
- Single sink preventing really hygienic washing up – there is nowhere to rinse the plates in hot water if the sink is full.
- Narrow gaps between units have become dirt traps.
- Four cats living and eating with the family.
- Saucepans stored on open shelves at floor . . . and cat level.
- Crockery left on an open drainer after it has dried.
- Wooden implements which can harbour dirt and bacteria.
- Two chopping boards (one for raw meat, the other for cooked) to avoid cross-contamination . . . the pity is they are stacked one on top of the other!
- Cat food next to the toaster.
- Garden chemicals on top of cupboard above food preparation area.
- Plants in food preparation area.
- Formica top is stained and blemished and requires renewal.

However Annette is an exceptional cook because she knows these things are wrong and intends to put them right. In fact there is much that she has already got right:

- First aid cabinet, including blue plasters which show up better if they fall into food.

- Fire extinguisher and blanket mounted on the wall.
- Use of drainer rather than tea towel.
- Use of colour-coded chopping boards for different purposes.
- Gas cooker on wheels allowing frequent cleaning around and behind.
- A covered vegetable storage rack.
- A small, cleanable pedal bin needing daily emptying.
- Nailbrush and soap for thorough cleansing of the hands; anti-bacterial cleaner for wiping work surfaces.
- Closed cupboards for crockery.

The major task Annette has set herself is knocking down the partition between the scullery and the dining room and completely redesigning the layout of her kitchen. In doing so she is going to employ the principles laid down for commercial kitchens in the Food Hygiene Regulations (1970). We have summarised those regulations for you opposite. And while considering them, we thought you would enjoy looking at a plan of Annette's house before and after (pages 132 and 133). See if you can spot the crucial differences and deduce the purpose of the changes. Annette is the first to point out that some of her plans are tentative and depend on an adequate supply of funds!

You do not need to study the difference between the two plans for long before the careful thinking behind the idea becomes apparent. A few RSJs and several thousands of pounds later you can see a kitchen that – as far as possible – allows you to work from the 'dirty' near the door to the 'clean' at the serving end of the cooking process with as little back-tracking as possible. This approach drastically cuts down the opportunities for cross-contamination.

We considered do's and don'ts in the average kitchen quite carefully in Chapters 4 and 5. But it is interesting to reconsider some of those rules in terms of kitchen design. Many of these are outlined in the Food Hygiene Regulations (1970) for those who are building commercial kitchens, and all are accepted as good practice. Some may seem rather extreme for domestic kitchens, but they all exemplify useful lessons.

Storage

All food materials likely to harbour bacteria – particularly meat, fruit and vegetables – should be stored near the door. They should not be carried across the kitchen. Cupboards (not bare wood) should have doors so that all utensils and crockery are covered.

Lighting

In a word, this should be bright. Good lighting makes dirt easier to detect and can deter vermin. Light fittings should be easy to clean and vapour-resistant. Windows should preferably be north-facing to cut down on direct sunlight and therefore excess heat. Higher windowsills above work surfaces are less likely to collect dirt.

Walls and ceilings

Walls should be covered with material that is impervious and easy to clean, preferably up to a height of six feet. Tiles are a good idea. Wall paint must be oil-based or silk-finish emulsion for the same reasons. Ceilings should be white to reflect the light.

Floors

These must again be smooth, impervious and easy to clean. They should be light to show up the dirt. The material used should not become slippery when wet. An additional idea – the floor covering could be curved up to all cupboards and walls, leaving no gaps for dirt to collect in.

Ventilation

This must be efficient to get rid of steam and grease and to keep the heat down.

Cross-contamination

Work surfaces should be impervious and easy to clean – and this rules out wood. Separate chopping boards and knives should be used for raw meat (colour-coding is a good idea). Many commercial kitchens have separate fridges for raw and

KITCHEN LAYOUT BEFORE

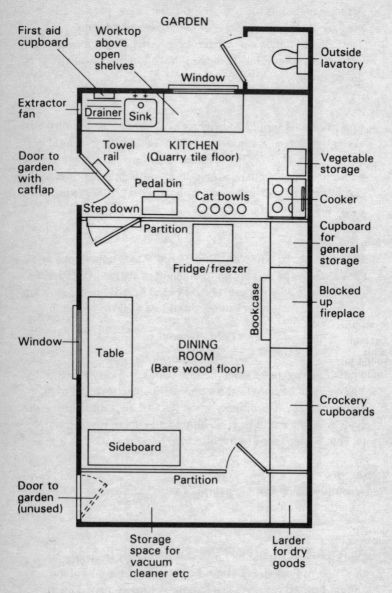

KITCHEN LAYOUT AFTER

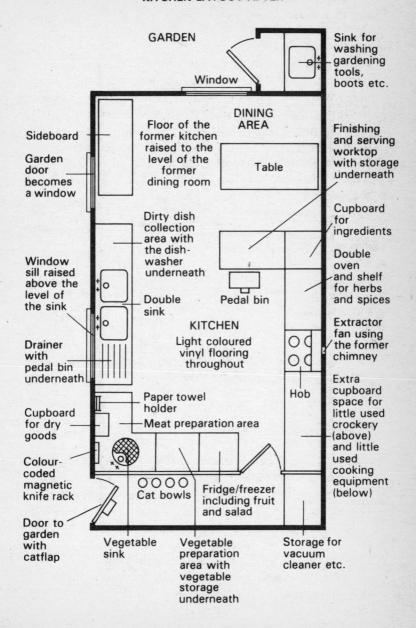

GARDEN

Window

Sink for washing gardening tools, boots etc.

DINING AREA

Table

Floor of the former kitchen raised to the level of the former dining room

Sideboard

Garden door becomes a window

Finishing and serving worktop with storage underneath

Cupboard for ingredients

Dirty dish collection area with the dish-washer underneath

Double oven and shelf for herbs and spices

Window sill raised above the level of the sink

Double sink

Pedal bin

KITCHEN

Light coloured vinyl flooring throughout

Extractor fan using the former chimney

Drainer with pedal bin underneath

Paper towel holder

Hob

Extra cupboard space for little used crockery (above) and little used cooking equipment (below)

Cupboard for dry goods

Meat preparation area

Colour-coded magnetic knife rack

Cat bowls

Fridge/freezer including fruit and salad

Door to garden with catflap

Vegetable sink

Vegetable preparation area with vegetable storage underneath

Storage for vacuum cleaner etc.

cooked foods. Cross-contamination, as we have seen, is a very
common cause of food poisoning.

Washing-up

It is easy to forget that we wash up not only to remove food
particles but also to kill bacteria. To achieve the latter, water
needs to be hotter than the hand can bear – the ideal answer is
therefore a dishwasher. Failing this, a double sink is required.
Stack the dirty plates on the right-hand draining board, wash
them in the right-hand sink, rinse them for two minutes in very
hot water in the left-hand sink and then leave them to dry
stacked on the left-hand draining board. Tea towels are banned
because they harbour bacteria. The classic order for washing-
up is:

- glasses
- silver
- knives
- cleanest china
- dirtiest china
- and saucepans.

On completion clean the sink thoroughly and fill the U-bend
with *cold* water (to deter bacterial growth).

The sink

The sink must only be used for food-related activities, not for
floor buckets and suchlike. Handwashing should be done in
a separate hand basin. Hand towels (like tea towels) should
not be used – paper towels can be used instead. Dish cloths
should always be soaked overnight in bleach or some other
disinfectant.

Rubbish

Rubbish should be kept in a closed container, preferably foot-
operated. The bin should be kept at the 'dirty' end of the kitchen and must be emptied every day.

Vermin

Kitchens should be vermin-proof. All holes must be blocked and doors should be self-closing. Windows should have screens when open to keep flies out.

It has to be said that no one can afford the time or the money to run their domestic kitchen strictly along the lines of a commercial one. But there is still much we can learn from the professionals (or, at least, from the ones who have had the correct training and obey the rules). Annette Anderson may never be able to put her whole renovation plan into operation. But it is certain that the more of it she does implement the less likely she is to suffer from food poisoning.

8 Eating Out at Home and Abroad

Illness on holiday can be particularly worrying. Often if you are travelling in exotic places, standards of health care are not particularly good. And the extra stress involved in even a short-lived bout of food poisoning can ruin a holiday.

The Department of Health and the Central Office of Information do produce advice for travellers about health in two, recently updated booklets (SA40 and SA41). They are primarily concerned with more serious health issues such as Malaria, Aids and how to get medical attention. Surprisingly, the booklets give little or no advice on food and food hygiene except to say that Hepatitis A and Typhoid can be caught by consuming contaminated water and food. Travellers are merely advised to be careful about what they eat and drink. In this chapter we want to look at the problems of eating abroad and, where possible, give some rather more practical advice than that offered by the Government.

In Chapter 1, we listed popular names for food poisoning and noted how many echoed our colonial past or were associated with foreign travel. If results of a 1988 *Holiday Which?* survey are representative, little has changed. It covered hotels and restaurant kitchens from Tunisia, Majorca and Rhodes. Of 59 hotel kitchens visited, none were excellent and 14 were poor. (By poor, it was considered that they had hygiene problems that were bad enough to lead to an outbreak of food poisoning.) Of 17 food samples taken from restaurants, no fewer than 10 contained the faecal organism Escherichia coli. This indicated very poor standards of handling and personal hygiene.

The year before (May 1987) *Holiday Which?* published another revealing survey. They asked their members how many of them had been ill during either of their last two foreign holidays. A total of 23000 people responded and the results are shown below. Note that these figures cover *all* illnesses, not just food poisoning. However we all know that the most common ailment when abroad is a stomach upset. So the experiences of the Consumers' Association members are still very instructive.

COUNTRY VISITED	PERCENTAGE SUFFERING ILLNESS	SIZE OF SAMPLE
Egypt	56	144
India and Nepal	50	236
Gambia	46	94
Turkey	41	297
Kenya, Tunisia	34	156, 234
Morocco	29	285
South-East Asia	28	202
USSR, Bulgaria	22	139, 112
Portugal	18	2162
Greece, Spain	16	3991, 8909
Malta	15	525
Yugoslavia, Caribbean	14	1012, 284
Israel	12	229
France, Cyprus, USA, Italy	9	7887, 608, 1458, 2295
Austria	7	1509
Switzerland, Scandinavia, Canada	6	1133, 609, 422
West Germany	5	1236
Eire, Belgium	4	413, 346
Netherlands	3	739

Wherever you go on holiday you are more likely to suffer a stomach upset in the first few days. The body's immune system is affected by such things as stress, a change of normal routine and excess sun and alcohol. It is therefore less able to fight infection. For this reason it's always worth taking things easy for the first few days, eating and drinking sensibly until you've settled in.

We obviously cannot go through all the menus you're

likely to encounter in every country. So the following precautions are only a general guide:

- Choose a restaurant or café that looks clean and busy. Front-of-house cleanliness is a reasonable guide to back-of-house standards and a busy restaurant will also have a fast turnover of food.
- If you are not sure about standards, choose low-risk menu items that are likely to receive high-temperature cooking. Remember, anything 'wet cooked' (such as fried or grilled) is likely to be safer than slower-cooked food. Solid pieces of meat like steaks, chops and kebab cubes are also safer than minced meat dishes. Fresh fish, especially if grilled or fried, will generally be safe. Most cooked vegetables, including chips, will be fine.
- In certain countries, or areas where water supplies are suspect, salads should be avoided. In the *Which?* survey, salads were often found to be contaminated with faecal organisms.
- Avoid filter-feeding shellfish unless you're absolutely certain they have been harvested from waters that are free of pollution. (They include cockles, mussels and oysters.)
- Drink bottled beer, soft drinks or mineral waters from glass bottles if you're not sure about the quality of the drinking water. Despite recent incidents in Cornwall and elsewhere, British tap water is still among the cleanest in the world and very few countries come up to our standards.
- Only drink pasteurised milk and milk products. Buy ice-cream that is obviously made by a commercial company. With individual street vendors you will be taking something of a risk.
- Watch out for buffets where food has been displayed for many hours at warm temperatures. You should certainly avoid any food that you saw on the buffet the day before.

But above all, don't be over-sensitive – the last thing we want to do is spoil anyone's holiday.

If you've read this book carefully you will have acquired some of the skills of an Environmental Health Officer. We now invite you to look at the following menu from a typical Greek taverna and decide which are the safest options.

M E N U

—— KALAMARI ——

Fried squid, served with chips and salad.

—— GRILLED FISH OF THE DAY ——

Fresh fish grilled over charcoal,
served with chips and salad.

—— DOLMADES ——

Vine leaves stuffed with
spiced minced meat and garlic.

—— MOUSSAKA ——

Minced meat and aubergine topped with a choice
of cheese or plain white sauce.

—— DONER KEBAB ——

Spiced minced meat skewered and cooked on a
spit, served in thin slices with pitta bread
and salad.

—— SOUVLAKIA ——

Small cubes of meat (choice of lamb, beef or pork)
skewered with vegetables and grilled over
charcoal.

. . .

Well, did you choose? These are our choices, and the reasons why.

Kalamari and grilled fish

This is definitely the safest option. Fish, as we learnt earlier, is much less likely to contain harmful bacteria in the first place. In addition, it has received high-temperature cooking for a short time.

These options are also accompanied by relatively safe food – chips and salad. There is a risk from salads, as we've already indicated. But that illustrates the point we made earlier – you've got to eat something. All we are suggesting is that you avoid the really obvious risks, particularly in the early days of your holiday.

Dolmades and moussaka

These are two other favourites and ones to avoid unless the dishes have been made up freshly. With minced meat, the outside of the joint, often contaminated, is mixed up with the more protected inner parts. If it's been left hanging around, particularly from morning to evening, then it's best avoided. (Both these dishes are often made up in advance and left standing until ordered and then reheated.)

Doner kebab

Perhaps the riskiest of all! The minced sliced meat (originally a Turkish speciality) is handled a lot during preparation of the doner kebab and there are many opportunities for contamination. Also, the continual reheating and cooling of a large piece of skewered meat creates the ideal conditions for bacterial growth, especially inside the kebab. The kebabs are usually fairly large and can take a day or more to use up.

Finally, it's very easy for the chef to accidentally slice off undercooked meat as he's slicing off the surface cooked parts. Doner kebabs can be delicious but on holiday, with many other things to enjoy, make it a case of thanks, but no thanks.

Souvlakia

Unminced meat has fewer chances of being contaminated. And the hot grill which cooks the meat fiercely shortly before consumption denies the bugs any opportunity to multiply.

To sum up, one of the whole points of going abroad is to experience new foods. It would be a tragedy to go on holiday and only eat food you could have had at home. The advice we have given therefore really only relates to the early part of your holiday, unless you are particularly vulnerable to stomach upsets.

EATING OUT IN BRITAIN

It should be rather safer at home, shouldn't it? But general outbreaks of food poisoning mainly occur in restaurants and hotels. To a large extent, the consumer is forced to accept standards of hygiene in commercial premises without question. There is certainly no statutory right to inspect a restaurant kitchen and, although you could always ask, it is not usually practical to make regular excursions into the chef's domain.

For the most part we have to rely on our own observation of the dining area. And the following checklist should help you judge whether a restaurant's hygiene standards are as they should be:

- Tablecloths, cutlery and glasses should be spotlessly clean and in good condition.
- Waiters and waitresses should show high standards of personal hygiene.
- Hot food should be served *hot* on *hot* plates. Remember, lukewarm food is ideal for bacterial growth and survival. Likewise, cold food should be really cold.
- Don't accept obviously undercooked food (though some types of meat – beef and lamb – are served rare as a matter of choice). The point is that chicken and pork should always be well cooked.
- Unrefrigerated sweet trolleys are a menace. Fresh cream cakes, gateaux and the like are left unrefrigerated for hours on end

during lunchtime and evening sittings, allowing ample opportunity for bacterial growth.

■ Toilets should be spotlessly clean and provided with hand basins, hot water, soap, and roller or paper towels. (An interesting point here is that hot air hand dryers are not necessarily as hygienic as their manufacturers often claim. You might ask yourself where they draw their air from. Of course it's the toilet area. So guess what's blown all over your clean hands by the warm air dryer!)

However, even if you think you have been poisoned by a restaurant meal it can be risky to jump to conclusions. In their capacity as consultants to the food industry, the Food Hygiene Bureau were called to investigate a suspected case of food poisoning by a client who ran a national chain of well-known restaurants. On the face of it, things looked pretty bad for the Bureau's client. A family party of eight people had eaten Sunday lunch at the restaurant and by 6 p.m. the first member of the party had become ill. Over the next 12 hours everyone had fallen ill, some seriously, some less so.

However the Bureau's consultant Environmental Health Officer could not understand how the restaurant could have been responsible. Standards in the kitchen were extremely high. Furthermore, 250 other guests had been fed the same food the same day and not one had complained of illness.

The consultant decided to investigate further. After speaking to members of the party he discovered that they had also eaten together on the Saturday evening at a family barbecue. The food had consisted of sausages, beefburgers and chicken (all high-risk foods), which had been only partially cooked because the barbecue had been rained off. Although it was suggested that the food had been 'finished off' in the host's kitchen, the incubation period (the time between eating the food and developing symptoms) and the high standards at the restaurant suggested the barbecue was much more likely to have caused the family's illness.

As this story shows, most people, if they suffer food poisoning, assume that the last meal they ate must have been the cause. This is usually because it's also the meal they have violently consigned to the toilet. However incubation periods can be as long as a week for some types of food poisoning and food-borne illness (see Chapter 9, page 147).

If you do ever end up with diarrhoea or vomiting there can be many many different causes, not least too much alcohol. So it is worth making a few enquiries yourself before you involve an Environmental Health Officer. Perhaps the most obvious thing to do is to look for any common foods – that's to say foods that everyone who has been ill has eaten. Secondly, if the food has been prepared at home, think back over the preparation, and see if any mistakes were made regarding temperature control or other important areas of food hygiene.

Once you've asked a few of these simple questions, if you still feel that food produced by someone else was responsible, then it's definitely worth giving the Environmental Health Officer a call.

Take-away fast food

Like supermarkets, many fast food chains have invested heavily in high standards of hygiene. Their investment in national and even international brand names ensures that the public recognise their products wherever they may be. Of course the down side of such a strong brand identity is that any food scare or adverse publicity affects an entire brand, not just the restaurant or take-away concerned. Commendably, some leading companies have built hygiene into their operations. It is an integral part of their management system and the results of such a positive attitude are there for all to see.

In terms of food hygiene, most fast food is relatively safe. It is prepared on demand, often subjected to high-temperature cooking methods and eaten straight away. However, at the other end of the scale, there are the local burger and kebab take-aways or mobile suppliers. Frankly, standards in this type of operation vary so dramatically that the best advice is simply to look at the interior of the van and its operator, particularly his or her hands, and ask yourself the simple question, is this van and person clean? Do I want to eat this food?

van and person clean? Do I want to eat this food?

Despite our best efforts, most of us will experience food poisoning at some point. The next chapter gives advice on what to do if you get ill and suspect it may be 'something you've eaten'.

9 IF YOU DO GET ILL ...

The purpose of this book is prevention not cure. But if, through no fault of your own, you do get food poisoning then we do not want to leave you suffering helplessly. And anyway, if your case of food poisoning can be confirmed and dealt with, many others may be prevented ...

As we have seen, the vast majority of food poisoning cases remain undiagnosed and unrecognised, either because we nurse ourselves through them or because our doctor does not take them any further. But there is, in fact, a large official body whose job it is to investigate food poisoning. If you get ill and you fear it might be food poisoning your local Environmental Health Officer would like to hear from you and can be contacted through your local council.

This chapter gives advice on what to do if you become ill. Specifically:

- how to spot possible food poisoning – its usual symptoms and causes
- how to treat it – first aid
- how to report it and have it investigated
- and how Environmental Health Officers go about their investigations.

HOW TO SPOT FOOD POISONING

Food poisoning generally lasts between one and three days and the most common symptom is literally a gut reaction – diarrhoea. Other symptoms include nausea, vomiting, abdominal cramps, passing blood, headaches, fever, tiredness and even depression. Despite this frightening catalogue, it is not normally a serious affliction. But very severe cases can be fatal, particularly if the sufferer is old, very young or already unwell.

Food poisoning often happens sporadically, as an isolated incident with a single victim. But of course epidemics do occur, whether in a household, an institution or among the clientele of a restaurant.

An attack may strike us within an hour of eating contaminated food but it can be as much as five days before we are aware of any symptoms. In Chapter 3 we explained that there are many harmless bacteria already in our stomachs, helping with our digestion. A smaller number of bacteria types are harmful to us (see opposite) but only if consumed in sufficient quantities. For instance, with Salmonella most of us would normally need to eat at least 100000 organisms to suffer any unpleasant symptoms. (Since one Salmonella bacterium can multiply to 11 million in eight hours at room temperature it is not too difficult to eat a million!)

Assume you have just eaten one million Salmonella bacteria in a badly cooked piece of chicken. What happens in your gut is this: the Salmonella, faced by competition from the harmless bacteria already there and the hostility of your stomach acid, are gradually killed off. As the bacteria die they release a toxin which upsets your alimentary canal. And that is when the familiar symptoms appear.

But there are a number of other reasons why you might suffer such symptoms. For instance:

■ gastric flu
■ nervousness
■ shock
■ or over-indulgence in alcohol.

Not every upset stomach is a case of food poisoning.

In any event, while the symptoms of food poisoning may last no longer than three days, you might actually feel unwell for a week or longer. It takes us a little while to recover from what is a rather unpleasant trauma.

There are many different groups of bacteria which are known to cause food poisoning and each organism produces slightly different symptoms. An analysis of these can help detect which of the bugs has got a grip on our vitals. The four ways they might vary are:

- incubation period
- physical symptoms
- duration of symptoms
- and actual cause of illness (some bacteria upset the stomach by sheer force of numbers; others, like Salmonella, by releasing toxins as they die; and others by releasing toxins in the food before it is consumed).

Here, we describe eight types of bacteria. Some are relatively common and others are quite rare but still well known because of the publicity they have recently received. (For further details you can turn back to Chapter 3, page 42.)

Salmonella

There are 2000 strains of Salmonella. It is present in much of the poultry we buy and has been found increasingly in eggs – albeit in small numbers so far. As we have said, it produces toxins in our gut. These can cause diarrhoea, nausea, vomiting, headaches, fever and aching limbs. The incubation period is anything from six hours to two days, depending on the strain and the number of bacteria present. You can take up to a week to recover.

Campylobacter

There are even more confirmed cases of Campylobacter poisoning than of Salmonellosis (see Chapter 2, page 36). The symptoms tend to be more unpleasant and longer-lasting too. They can include severe stomach pains and the passing of blood with diarrhoea. The incubation period is two to five days. No toxin is involved – the bacteria in this case inflame the stomach wall.

Staphylococcus aureus

This is another commonly found bacterium. It can thrive in meats such as ham and bacon which other bugs find too salty.

It also likes milk and uncooked milk products. One of its most common sources is our own body – it can exist in our noses, in spots and cuts on our skins. It may not cause us any problems in our noses but when transferred carelessly to food (say, via the hands after nose-blowing) it can multiply rapidly at room temperature. The incubation period is between two and six hours and symptoms include vomiting, diarrhoea and abdominal pains. Although it can result in complete collapse an attack tends to last only 24 hours.

Clostridium perfringens

This is a less common source of food poisoning but it is still widespread in soil. It has an incubation period of eight to 22 hours and lasts between 12 and 24 hours. Symptoms include abdominal pain, nausea and diarrhoea but not usually vomiting. Once again, it releases a toxin in our gut.

Bacillus cereus

Bacillus cereus may exist in small quantities in a number of cereals. If they are not washed thoroughly it can propagate, particularly when the conditions are right. It loves warm rice that has been sitting around for a while – a particular danger with take-away foods. The incubation period is one to six hours. The symptoms are violent but brief – intense vomiting and the possibility of diarrhoea, normally lasting just a day. In this case the bacterium produces a toxin in the rice itself. The incubation period is so short because the toxin hits the gut immediately.

Vibro parahaemolyticus

This is also less common and occurs in shellfish and other seafood. The incubation period can be anything from two to 48 hours, but it is usually about 15 hours. The symptoms are severe: vomiting, diarrhoea and fever lasting between two and five days. An attack can take some time to recover from.

Listeria monocytogenes

As yet Listeriosis is thought to be relatively rare. (Just how rare is debatable – see Chapter 2, page 37.) Listeria is commonly found in soil, water and the guts of animals. When it enters our bodies – whether in unwashed vegetables, unhygienically prepared cook-chill meals or soft cheese – most of us are able to cope because we have an inbuilt resistance (indeed some of us carry it in our gut permanently and suffer no ill-effects). But people with lowered immunity can contract Listeriosis. Examples of those at risk are pregnant women, babies, the elderly and the sick (particularly Aids sufferers and cancer patients). The incubation period can last up to several weeks and the symptoms are very like those of flu – a temperature and dizziness. Listeriosis can lead to miscarriages, meningitis and even death.

Clostridium botulinium

This is another very serious form of food poisoning. But it is extremely rare in this country – we have had only one recorded case of 'botulism' in Britain over the past few years. It is to be found in unhygienically canned or bottled food and the incubation period is 24 to 48 hours. The bacteria attack the nervous system and although diarrhoea may occur at first it can then be replaced by constipation. Other symptoms are fatigue, headaches, dizziness, vision and speech difficulties, paralysis and coma. It can easily prove fatal. Death often occurs within a day to a week and survivors may take as much as six months to recover. The bacteria produce toxins in the contaminated food.

HOW TO TREAT IT – FIRST AID

There are two very simple overriding pieces of advice here:

- *If the symptoms persist for more than 24 hours consult your doctor.*

- *If the symptoms are particularly severe or the sufferer is elderly, very young, pregnant or already ill, consult a doctor as soon as possible.*

The Department of Health does not issue a leaflet on how to handle food poisoning because it believes the advice given above is the crucial thing to know. But in the meantime there are some commonsense measures to help you and your body through an attack of food poisoning. It is most important:

■ to rest your upset stomach
■ and to keep up your fluid levels.

The obvious way to rest your upset stomach – to give your disturbed alimentary tract a break – is not to eat. Initially you will not feel like eating anyway. But when the worst is over, and you want to eat again, start with small quantities and avoid fatty foods. Vomiting and diarrhoea are the body's ways of ridding itself of poison – unwelcome bacteria or the toxins they produce. So however unpleasant the symptoms, it is normally better to endure them instead of immediately taking some medicine to 'bind' you up again. But if the diarrhoea or vomiting become chronic then your doctor may choose to prescribe something to stop it. You may also need to stop the symptoms prematurely if you have to travel. Otherwise, let your body destroy the bacteria and toxins, and excrete them as nature intended.

While that admittedly unpleasant process is taking place you will be losing vast amounts of liquid and minerals that your system would normally retain. So there are dangers of dehydration and loss of essential minerals. These dangers are more acute for young children, the elderly and those who are already ill. To cope with dehydration, anyone with food poisoning should try to drink a large glassful or around half a pint of liquid every two hours. Water is fine but to replace minerals there are a number of rehydrating solutions you can buy at the chemist that usually come in the form of powders. They chiefly contain a mixture of glucose, potassium and sodium chloride (salt). Here are the names of some of the more common products:

■ Rehydrat sachets
■ Electrolade sachets
■ Dioralyte sachets.

Some of the powders come in different flavours. You can, of course, make up your own solution: 1 litre of water, 8 teaspoons of sugar and 1 teaspoon of salt. This is commonly used to help sick children in the Third World.

When the symptoms become less severe you can progress to mild food such as clear soup and dry bread.

During the period of illness you will have been excreting vast numbers of harmful bacteria in your faeces. But you may not realise that even when you feel fully recovered you will continue to excrete the offending bacteria. After you are better you can *still* infect others in the house. So while you are ill, and for a few days afterwards, observe these simple rules:

- If possible, do not handle or prepare foods for others.
- In any event, wash your hands thoroughly with soap and hot water, particularly after you have been to the lavatory.
- Use strong disinfectant to clean surfaces and utensils with which you have been in contact, especially in the bathroom and kitchen. (For further details on disinfectants you can turn to Chapter 5, page 88.)
- Wash your sheets and towels in hot water – economy and low-temperature washes may not kill organisms. Tumble drying at high temperatures can.

Some of us are classed by Environmental Health Officers as 'high risk' – that is, as representing a special risk to others. If you belong to any of these groups then it is very important that you are cleared by an Environmental Health Officer before you return to your place of work. Examples are:

- Water workers, who might contaminate drinking water.
- Food handlers who touch unwrapped foods which will be consumed raw or without further cooking. (Health officials would like to extend this to *all* food handlers but, surprisingly, that is not how the law stands at the moment.)
- Health care and nursery staff who have direct contact with people or who serve food.
- Medical staff such as doctors, nurses and dentists.

■ Children aged less than five who attend nurseries or playgroups. (Their standards of personal hygiene will be much lower than older children.)

■ Others whose standards of personal hygiene are likely to be low such as the mentally and physically disabled, and the elderly.

There are two other groups whom the experts regard as posing a high risk to the rest of us. They are known as 'carriers' and 'excreters'.

Carriers

Bacteria which cause food poisoning can be *carried* by some people who do not suffer any symptoms but who are quite able to contaminate food, utensils, towels and so on. These are 'carriers'. Chronic carriers are more commonly women than men, and the risk of becoming one increases after the age of 30.

The classic case was Mary Mallon, a cook in New York before the First World War. Unbeknown to anyone, she was a carrier of Typhoid. When she was finally diagnosed by New York City health officials in 1914 they estimated that she had caused 1344 cases of Typhoid – a large number of them resulting in death. Despite the carnage of her culinary career she was given the almost affectionate nickname of 'Typhoid Mary'. To persuade her to give up cooking the City Health Department voted Typhoid Mary a pension and ordered her to report regularly to them so as to ensure she had not escaped the city and set up a deadly 'diner' somewhere else. She lived quite happily with her pension and her Typhoid bacteria until her death (from natural causes) in 1938.

Excreters

'Excreters' are those who continue to excrete the harmful bacteria after their own recovery (for less than 12 months; you become a 'carrier' after 12 months). As many as five per cent of Typhoid sufferers become temporary carriers of the bacterium and may continue to excrete the organism for as long as 12 months afterwards. Often the excretion is intermittent which makes them very difficult to detect. The danger, of course, is that excreters will spread harmful bacteria without knowing it. They represent a particular danger if they are in one of the high-risk groups.

Not long ago an 'excreter' was found to be responsible for an outbreak of Salmonella typhimurium in a mental hospital. He was then examined regularly over a 20-month period – four faeces samples were taken and analysed every month. For a whole six months during this period the tests were negative and there was no danger of him spreading the bug. Then the Salmonella typhimurium appeared again. In the end he was cleared but until then he represented quite a danger to the mental patients he would have been caring for.

Whether you are a member of one of the high-risk groups or merely live at home with your family, the dangers posed by food poisoning are considerable. That is why, if you think you have food poisoning, it is well worth taking the matter further.

How to report it

Before we look at how to report a suspected case of food poisoning we should consider why most cases go unreported and ask whether it is in fact worth reporting them. As we mentioned in Chapter 2, experts believe there may be two million cases of Salmonella poisoning a year, the majority of which will have been contracted through food. Yet only a tiny fraction of those cases are reported and investigated, and an even smaller number become confirmed cases. We also discussed the many reasons why so many food poisoning incidents – whether from Salmonella or some other cause – are not reported. Victims may not realise what has happened or they may simply nurse themselves at home, and if they go to the doctor he may not bother to report it. (He has a legal duty to report 'notifiable diseases' of which food poisoning is one, indeed he even gets over £1 for filling out the form. But so many cases are uncertain, particularly if none of the suspect food is left to analyse.)

Our attitudes to food poisoning are further elucidated by a very revealing survey carried out by the Ministry of Agriculture, Fisheries and Food and published quietly in 1988. They polled 2000 adults across Britain and discovered that:

■ Only 11 per cent generally regarded the home as a likely source of food poisoning. (Suspicion centred instead on 'foreign' restaurants in particular, and take-aways in general.)
■ Although 43 per cent reported having had an upset stomach in the previous six months only 4 per cent of all those polled attributed it to food. (Much more popular culprits were 'germs, viruses or bugs' and alcoholic drinks.)
■ Among the 4 per cent who actually thought they had suffered food poisoning, the vast majority once again blamed eating out and only a minority singled out food prepared in the home.

Let us compare those *opinions* – for that is what they are – with what we know to be the case. An analysis by the Department of Health in 1985, carried out on 463 outbreaks of food poisoning, showed that 259 were traced to the home and only 64 to restaurants. So more than half occurred in the home and fewer than a seventh occurred in restaurants . . . a very different story.

We have no figure for how many upset stomachs can be blamed on food poisoning. But we do know that there are hundreds of thousands, if not millions, of cases and we can be sure that as a proportion of all stomach upsets they must be vastly higher than 4 per cent.

There is one more statistic that is worth extracting from the Government survey at this stage: the 4 per cent who actually attributed their upset stomachs to food poisoning were a tiny number – actually only 75 of those polled. But how many of them reported the incident to their doctors or local Environmental Health Office? Only 30, or just two-fifths. So even when we strongly believe we have suffered from food poisoning we are most likely to do nothing about it. It is fair to assume that we do not realise how reporting could benefit us and others. Nor do we actually know how to go about reporting. This section aims to put that right. First, what are some of the benefits of having an investigation? A number of discoveries could be made:

- There may be something wrong with your kitchen, such as a contaminated work surface or malfunctioning piece of equipment like a warm fridge.
- You may have cooked some food incorrectly and you could learn the right way.
- You may be found to be a 'carrier' or an 'excreter' and therefore a danger to your family unless precautions are taken.
- Your local shop may be supplying you with bad food because of some fault in its operation or its suppliers.
- You may have eaten a food product which is contaminated and could be taken off the shelves, saving others from illness.
- Bad practices or malfunctioning machinery might be discovered at a restaurant or take-away where you have been.

So, yes, it must be worth reporting a suspected case of food poisoning or encouraging your doctor to do so. But what about the workload for the hospitals and Public Health Laboratories who test the samples and the Environmental Health Officers who carry out the investigation? If several hundred thousand extra cases were suddenly reported to them would they be able to cope? The short answer is no.

Environmental Health Officers (or EHOs as they are known) are responsible for public health, housing and the environment (i.e. pollution) as well as food. In 1989 they report being under strength by 400 across the country. But even if they were up to strength in the official sense they would still be woefully short of the manpower they need to tackle Britain's epidemic of food poisoning seriously. The key to tackling food poisoning is prevention – that is the underlying principle of this book. But, as things stand, EHOs admit they can mostly only react to food poisoning *after* it has occurred. They cannot chase the public and the food catering industry to improve their practices *before* outbreaks happen.

EHOs are brave souls and they say they would love many more members of the public to report suspected cases of food poisoning. But to prevent them being overwhelmed by a flood of cases that may not be food poisoning, or that are near-impossible to investigate, you might ask yourself these two questions:

■ Is my upset stomach likely to have been caused by something I ate or is there some other probable cause? (For instance, I drank too much alcohol, I am very worried or nervous about something at the moment, I am in the early stages of preg-nancy, or my doctor advises me I have another ailment altogether such as gastric flu.)
■ Is any of the suspect food still around – either in the cooked dish or as unused raw material? (If so, the job of detection will be very much easier.)

We should make it clear, however, that this does not affect the basic advice given earlier in this chapter about consulting your doctor (see page 149). These two questions really amount to using your common sense and keeping a sense of proportion.

Reporting a case of food poisoning

If you are satisfied that there is what lawyers call a 'prima facie' case (a case to answer) then you can have it reported via your doctor whom you may have already consulted anyway. Or you can telephone your local Environmental Health Office via your local council. (EHOs are employed by local councils.) You should always call the EHO as soon as possible so that the maximum amount of evidence is still available. You will be put through to the Infectious Diseases Clerk or an EHO who will ask you a number of questions so they can fill in a case card. They will ask:

■ what your symptoms are
■ why you think it may be food poisoning
■ when you started to feel ill
■ what you have eaten in the last 24 to 48 hours
■ what your job is and where you work.

The next step – as long as the Health Office agrees that the case is worth investigating – is a visit from an EHO. Food poisoning is high priority for EHOs and they will normally visit the same day. It would be helpful for all of us to understand what evidence EHOs need to establish food poisoning. They are looking to confirm five factors:

- That an infecting organism is present in the kitchen, in food, on the food handler or in animals.
- That there was a means of transfer to the victim. The vehicle might be the food itself or contaminated work surfaces, utensils, cloths or other equipment.
- That the food in question is suitable for bacterial growth.
- That the conditions the food was stored in were favourable to bacteria (i.e. warm enough) for at least two hours.
- That the victim or victims are likely to have been made ill by the bacteria.

When an EHO visits you there is no reason to be apprehensive. He (or she) is just as much a professional as your doctor or dentist and will practise the same rules of confidentiality. The Officer will take samples of suspect food for analysis at your local Public Health Laboratory. Preferably they will want to take away food from the actual dish in question. If that is not possible – because it has been completely consumed or thrown away (though retrieve it from the dustbin if you can) – then they might ask to take samples from other unused raw food materials from the same shopping trip. They will be interested in inspecting kitchen equipment – chiefly the fridge – to see whether it is working properly. They will also want to examine work surfaces to see if they are contaminated. Of course this is not merely to advise you to replace your chopping board. They will be working out how bacteria might have spread from one food to another or from one area to another.

In order to pinpoint how an infection might have spread, the Officer will also want to question you about other people you have come into contact with recently, either because they may be the source of the problem or because you may have passed it on to them. Examples of contacts are other members of the household with whom you share the kitchen, the bedroom or the bathroom, colleagues at work, other children at school or boyfriends and girlfriends. As we have seen earlier in this chapter, an EHO has the power to prevent people who are not yet clear of infection from returning to work in certain institutions such as schools, hospitals and restaurants. In such circumstances compensation is available so it is always better to be completely open with the Officer. You might well be putting many others at risk otherwise, and you would probably be found out anyway.

Let us give you a real example. Not long ago a trained chef applied for a job in the canteen kitchen of a multinational oil company. He had had an upset stomach which he believed to be food poisoning just two weeks before. But he had not reported it to anyone. The company gave him a medical as part of their normal health screening procedure and he was found to be a Salmonella 'excreter'. He did receive compensation for loss of earnings but the company gave the job to someone else. They came to the conclusion that they did not want the sort of chef who would not make a full disclosure of food poisoning.

Once an EHO has considered your case and assessed the risk to others (by consulting Medical Officers) he may well ask you for a sample of your faeces for analysis. This is easily supplied but a word or two about it might set your mind at rest. The Officer will leave you with a small aluminium container and a spatula. In cases of severe diarrhoea you can use a chamber pot or similar receptacle which has been well washed with hot water beforehand. Place a piece of lavatory paper in the bottom and produce a specimen into the pot. Take *one* spoonful with the spatula and place it inside the aluminium container. There is no need to fill the container. Screw the top on tightly and then wash your hands. The aluminium container should then be sealed twice in the two plastic bags provided. If your faeces are not so loose then you can sit on the lavatory and produce them on to a piece of lavatory paper from which you can spoon your sample. Enter the date of the specimen on the examination form provided. The EHO will have either arranged to collect the specimen from you or have asked you to deliver it to their divisional office by 2 p.m. Results from the analysis usually come back in 48 hours.

If after an initial visit the Officer decides that the most likely culprit is a restaurant or a staff canteen then they will initiate similar procedures at that place. If they decide that a particular food product represents a threat to public health then they can consult the Department of Health's District Medical Officer. Once the Medical Officer and their officials are sure of the problem then they can issue a Food Hazard Warning and demand that the product be withdrawn from public sale. An example of this which received widespread publicity in 1988 was the case of the Pepperami salami sticks. These 'mini-salamis' were widely on sale at supermarket checkouts wrapped in distinctive green foil. After several outbreaks of Salmonella typhimurium in different areas the Pepperami was found to be the cause. Quite a few were harbouring Salmonella having been contaminated during manufacture. They were immediately withdrawn until new supplies were proven safe.

Apart from investigating individual cases Environmental Health Officers have an important role in liaising with family doctors, Medical Officers and Public Health Laboratories. It is the Public Health Laboratories who compile the weekly Communicable Disease Report we mentioned in Chapter 2. They rely on EHOs to inform them of cases of Salmonella and Campylobacter poisoning and other such communicable diseases.

EHOs have a vital role to play in fighting the food poisoning problems Britain now faces. They need all the help they can get and we should all be willing to contact them in the event of food poisoning in our own households. They may not always feel a visit is necessary. We may only see them once if the case is impossible to pin down or we may see them relatively often during the period of recovery from confirmed food poisoning. In any event they are public officials we should be more aware of. To give you a better idea of how they go about their work we have three real case studies.

Case 1: The Wedding

All EHOs say if you are hell-bent on contracting food poisoning you should go to a wedding. The catering is often done by amateurs such as members of the family. They will prepare the food a long time ahead and nearly always set it out well in advance, usually in a warm room. Then there are the inevitable delays. And here is the killer: the food itself is the sort that bacteria adore – chicken and other cold meats in particular.

Rachel Gold's family had organised a slap-up wedding for her and Jonathan. After the ceremony at the synagogue they had hired Sparklers restaurant and wine bar for the reception. It was costing a tidy sum but, after all, you only get married once (or so the rather out-of-date saying has it). Although there were various small delays on the day and the food was not eaten as early as they planned, everyone had a marvellous time. In particular, the weather was perfect – in fact it was one of the hottest and most humid days of the year. Rachel and Jonathan flew off to Venice and Rachel's parents went home tired, considerably poorer but very happy.

The newly weds were still on the plane when the groom began to vomit. The 'happy couple' were anything but . . . in fact, they both looked decidedly pale. Soon after landing Rachel fell ill as well. The two of them spent the next 10 days either in bed groaning or rushing to the bathroom. They both described their honeymoon as 'a nightmare'. Just to give you an idea of how bad it was . . . they did not consummate their marriage until three weeks after the ceremony. On their bed of pain they gave little thought to the guests back home. But there the situation was even worse.

A total of 119 guests fell ill, 14 of whom had to go to hospital. The incubation period was anything between six hours (that was all it took for poor Jonathan to succumb) to four and a half days. Most were ill for a week, a few for as long as a month. Their most common symptoms were vomiting, fever and stomach pains.

The first the local Environmental Health Office knew about it was when a local isolation hospital contacted the

Infectious Diseases Clerk to say they had a lady suffering from food poisoning after attending a wedding reception at Sparklers the day before. The same day an EHO visited Sparklers and spoke to the manager. He confirmed that some 150 people had attended, that they ate at 5 p.m. and that the food had been laid out at around 3.30 p.m. None of the food was left but he provided an exhaustive menu which included chicken, turkey, beef, ham, salmon, prawns, crab and various salads. The EHO inspected the kitchen which he found satisfactorily equipped and clean. The same day he was able to discover that the fish had been delivered the day before the reception and kept in the deep-freeze, and that the meat had been delivered in a refrigerated lorry and kept refrigerated until use. The food was all prepared on the morning of the reception, ready for eating at 3 p.m. As it turned out on the day, the food was not eaten until 5 p.m. And during the delay it was left at room temperature.

Over the next few days the Communicable Diseases Surveillance Centre prepared questionnaires to go out to the guests requesting details of the food they had eaten and what their symptoms were. Many were asked for faecal samples. The fishmongers, butchers and patisserie who supplied Sparklers were inspected and given a clean bill of health. Then the results came through – the guests had all been struck by Salmonella typhimurium. Five members of the restaurant staff were also found to be Salmonella-positive but there was no hard evidence that they were the root of the problem. Indeed, the restaurant had by now reopened without any further food poisoning among its clients. The mystery deepened . . . what could have caused such an outbreak?

Salmonella typhimurium can be air-borne, water-borne or food-borne. The EHO concluded that this case must be food-borne because of the number affected – all had attended a 'food-eating' gathering. He examined each food for the likelihood of its being contaminated. It could be the raw meat but the butcher was clear; it could be the shellfish but they'd been imported and would have been inspected at the port of entry; it could be the cream in the cakes but the patisserie was hygienic and no other customers of theirs had suffered; it could be the chickens (the majority of which have Salmonella in them) but this would have required bad handling by the Sparklers staff.

Indeed, the EHO was slowly coming to the conclusion that the fault lay with Sparklers – possibly not handling the food well in the first place (for instance undercooking the chicken so the Salmonella were not killed) compounded by not allowing it to cool enough and not refrigerating it prior to its late use on a very warm day.

The three most likely causes were therefore:

■ Bad kitchen hygiene – where raw food with Salmonella in it is allowed to cross-contaminate other food that will be eaten raw or only lightly cooked.
■ Inadequate cooking – where food such as frozen chicken (as used at Sparklers) is not defrosted completely and thus not cooked properly. The Salmonella then survives.
■ A Salmonella 'excreter' among the staff who did not wash their hands after going to the lavatory.

At Sparklers the food poisoning almost certainly arose in one, and possibly several, of those ways. The EHO decided he would prosecute Sparklers. You might think it sounds like a rather flimsy case because of the lack of hard evidence. But remember the reports of the 119 people who suffered, having all eaten the same food. And indeed, the EHO won his case when the Sparklers owner and manager pleaded guilty and were fined £500. The sting in the tale was that they had to pay the considerable legal costs.

There can be no doubt that Sparklers were much more careful about correct food handling thereafter. And we could say that the whole incident ended up being rather worse for the wine bar's reputation than it was for Rachel and Jonathan's love-life.

Case 2: The Goodbye Drink

If you have read Chapter 1 you may remember the case of the Local Authority architect in the London Borough of Barnet who fell ill after eating a salad in a local pub. There we told the story from his perspective. Now we can tell it from the point of view of his Environmental Health Officer, who just happened to have his office one floor down.

Chris Carabine is the principal EHO in Barnet. One Friday afternoon in July he was contacted with the news that there had been an outbreak of suspected food poisoning on the floor above. The victims had apparently had drinks and a bite to eat in a nearby pub to say goodbye to an architect who was leaving. 'It always seem to happen late on a Friday afternoon when you're just about to go home,' Chris complains. 'But you've got to deal with it immediately – it's all part of the job.'

Chris and his team saw some of those affected the same afternoon and recorded details of their symptoms. The incubation times ranged from half an hour to three and a half hours. The average was around two hours. 'Because everyone was ill so quickly you think to yourself that it's not going to be Salmonella – that takes longer. So you're thinking of bacteria which are quicker to have an effect like Bacillus cereus, or of chemical poisoning which also has a shorter incubation. But you can't assume anything . . . you have to investigate.'

One problem was that Chris was too late to get any specimens of vomit – those symptoms had gone even by the end of the afternoon. The victims did give faecal samples but, just to emphasise how quick an EHO needs to be, when these were analysed on the Monday they were clear.

Luckily the landlady at the pub, when she heard of the problems, very responsibly held on to the leftovers from that day's salad bar. She explained the procedures for food preparation and storage in her kitchen and everything seemed very satisfactory. Where was the problem? The laboratory answered that question. It was in the cold rice and pasta in the salad selection – a bacterium called Bacillus cereus had colonised the food. Bacillus exists in quite a few cereals and small numbers of the bacteria can survive cooking. If the food is eaten straight away there's no problem. But if stored for a while in conditions which are not cold enough it can propagate rapidly. Then, while still in the food, its spores open and release a toxin. That is why it affects the alimentary tract so fast.

A quick check of the pub's fridge found that it was defective, and the rice – which had been stored overnight – had been kept at a temperature greater than 10°C. The pasta had almost certainly been cross-contaminated at the time of cooking, possibly by being drained in the same colander. The fact that the weather was particularly warm that July did not help.

Chris Carabine talked to the brewery which owned the pub. He said that the fridge needed immediate servicing and should not be used for overnight storage in the meantime. He recommended that they have a fridge thermometer on the premises so that next time they would be able to spot when temperatures were not as low as they ought to be. Lastly, and most importantly, he suggested that the brewery send their staff on a brief food hygiene course. It is a frightening thought but many of those who prepare and serve food in pubs have had no hygiene training at all.

By the time Chris was able to give his recommendations to the brewery the victims had long since recovered. Bacillus cereus hits you quickly and the effect is generally short-lived. The architectural department of Barnet Borough Council was soon back to processing the loft-conversion plans of the good citizens of North London.

Chris and his colleagues also circulated local Chinese restaurants with a warning about Bacillus cereus. And just to make sure their message got home they even placed an excellent notice in the local Chinese newspaper.

Case 3: A teatime snack

The owner of the Acme Sandwich Company ('the best thing since sliced bread') had had a good idea. He would open a chain of sandwich bars selling upmarket American-style sandwiches filled with chicken in a variety of exotic sauces. They certainly caught on and business was both brisk and profitable. He kept costs down and quality up by preparing most of the sandwiches at his central premises.

Early in January 1989 an Infectious Diseases Clerk in an Environmental Health Office not far from one of the sandwich bars got a call from a local office worker. Anne Sparks had bought and eaten a chicken and yoghurt roll from Acme the previous afternoon. She had been sick all night and said that she still felt 'queasy'. The clerk filled in a case card and within 10 minutes an EHO was following it up. Anne's symptoms strongly suggested Staphylococcus aureus. Although this bacterium shows up in a faecal specimen, its presence is not always conclusive, and on this occasion Anne was not asked for one. In the absence of any remains of the roll the officer knew he would have to investigate the sandwich bar itself.

As chance would have it the Infectious Diseases Clerk received a call the same day from another woman who suspected she had been poisoned by food. She came from another part of the area and blamed it on a restaurant that she felt extremely unwell after visiting. After careful questioning by the EHO, though, it emerged that she had bought chicken sandwiches from a sandwich bar the previous day . . . and that it was another branch of Acme. Her symptoms, by the way, exactly matched those of Anne Sparks. The EHO went into action.

He contacted Acme's owner immediately and arranged to collect samples of the chicken. The Public Health Laboratory confirmed within 48 hours that the chicken was the source of the problem, and that the problem was indeed Staphylococcus aureus. The chicken sandwiches were immediately withdrawn from all the branches.

As investigations at the central production unit proceeded, 10 other complaints of food poisoning emerged from consumers of Acme's chicken sandwiches – some from branches in other areas altogether. The mystifying thing was that although it was confirmed that the chicken was the culprit it was not at all clear how it was being contaminated. The standards of hygiene and the equipment at the unit all appeared entirely satisfactory. So the officer turned his attention to the staff and made an interesting discovery.

The food handler whose job it was to pick the cooked chicken from the carcass had an infection on one of his hands. The lesions of the skin eruption were exposed – he was wearing no waterproof dressing and no gloves. The warm, moist chicken, which all came into contact with his wound, was a perfect breeding ground. And swabs taken from the wound confirmed the source of the Staphylococcus.

The investigations were not complete though. The EHO then discovered that the warm chicken, once prepared, waited in a warm kitchen and was then transferred to a warm car for transport to the various sandwich bars. The bacteria had ample chance to multiply . . . and multiply they had. Not exactly the acme of hygiene.

As a result the food handler was taken out of the kitchen until his hand had healed, all the staff were sent on a food hygiene course and the owner of the Acme Sandwich Company agreed to suspend business until he had bought a refrigerated van. In this instance he was not prosecuted because he acted promptly, and because the loss of business was considered punishment enough.

FOOD HYGIENE LAW

It is our GPs and EHOs who are at the forefront of the battle against food poisoning – the former have to treat it and the latter have to prevent it. Failing that, they have to stop it spreading or recurring. But behind these 'front-line troops' are the Public Health Laboratories, the network of District Medical Officers, the Ministries of Agriculture and Health and, of course, the hospitals and community health services.

There are a number of laws which go some way to giving this 'army' the powers they need:

- The Food Hygiene Regulations (1970) control the production of food and give the EHOs many of their powers. But the regulations do not cover the non-commercial production of food in our own homes – we are free to poison ourselves.
- The Public Health (Control of Disease) Act 1984 requires doctors to inform the authorities of any notifiable disease, of which confirmed food poisoning is an example.
- Public Health Regulations of 1968 and Nursery and Child

Minder Regulations of 1948 govern the exclusion of 'carriers' from institutions.

- The Food Act (1984) governs the sale of food for human consumption and allows EHOs to inspect certain premises and close them down with the approval of a magistrate's court.
- Slaughterhouses, dairies and poultry houses have their standards governed by other specific legislation.

So there we are. We have explored what it's like to suffer food poisoning, seen how widespread the problem is, learnt the safest way to prepare and serve food, looked at how to protect our families (at home and abroad) and discovered what the ideal kitchen of the future might look like. Now you know what to do if you suffer an attack of food poisoning – but if you have read the rest of this book carefully we hope you will never need to refer to this last chapter again.

We would like to stress one more thing – to follow the advice in this book you do not need to be a fanatic. Food safety is all about common sense and it is not an end in itself. The real goal is to help us enjoy our food. Happy eating.

INDEX